AF885137

JUROR #6

Juror #6

Five Weeks in the Box

Dan Hiland

JUROR #6. Copyright © 2020 by Dan Hiland. All rights reserved. Printed in the United States of America. No part of this book mat be reproduced or transmitted in any form or by any means, electronic or mechanical, including photocopying, recording, or by any information storage or retrieval system, without written permission from the publisher.
All Rights Reserved
ISBN 13: 9780996873321
Printed in the United States of America
First paperback edition
Front cover design by Alison White
Manufactured in the United States of America

Disclaimer: This is a work of non-fiction. The people and places mentioned in this memoir are real, but due to privacy concerns, I have substituted fictitious names for real ones.

Writing website: danhilandwrites.com
Music reviews website: writeofmusic.com

Dedicated to every juror who's ever served

"In Suits at common law, where the value in controversy shall exceed twenty dollars, the right of trial by jury shall be preserved..."

Seventh Amendment to the Bill of Rights

"Jury service honorably performed is as important in defense of our country, its Constitution and laws, and the ideals and standards for which they stand, as the service rendered by the soldier on the field of battle in time of war."

Judge George H. Boldt

"I'm not trying to change your mind. It's just that... we're talking about somebody's life here. We can't decide it in five minutes. Supposing we're wrong?"

Juror #8, in "Twelve Angry Men"

"Whin th' case is all over, the jury'll pitch th' testimony out iv the window, an consider three questions: 'Did Lootgert look as though he'd kill his wife? Did his wife look as though she ought to be kilt? Isn't it time we wint to supper?'"

Finley Peter Dunne

Opening Arguments

Friday, August 8

SO, THIS IS THE WAY it ends- without a bang, without a party, without the traditional farewells to friends and co-workers. I decide, after finishing a document for someone in Engineering, that it's time to leave this place. At 1:30, I talk to a lady in HR and surrender my office key. Then I walk down the hallway to a small, nondescript office to say goodbye to Mr. Big, the man who started The Company, twenty years earlier. I wonder what he'll say, after all the work I've done there, all the contributions I've made, everything we've done as a team to make the business successful. I knock on the door frame. He looks up from his paperwork.

"Hi," I say, extending a hand. "Thought I'd stop off and say goodbye. This is my last day."

"Oh," he says, poker-faced, shaking my hand, and wishing me good luck. Then he returns to his paperwork.

Next, I'm off to tell Polly Pot (my boss). I've been keeping it a secret from her, due to our complicated relationship: I can't stand her, and she wants me fired. But so far, she hasn't been able to come up with a compelling enough reason. I knock at her door.

"Hi, Polly."

"Oh, *hello* Dan." She's all smiles- on the outside.

"Well, today's my last day. I know I was supposed to leave next week, but-"

"Oh, *really*? That's *too bad*."

I give her a questioning look, positive she's doing cartwheels in her head.

"And I was planning a farewell party for you," she says, pouty.

This, in itself, is reason enough to get the hell out of Dodge.

"Well, goodbye and good luck," she says, still all smiles as we shake hands and I exit, stage right.

I return the digital camera to Quality Assurance and show an inspector there how to use it. As I walk through the plant, I see documents taped or stuck to the sides of the machines- paperwork I created as a technical writer, over a twelve-year period. Paperwork full of photos and easy-to-understand instructions, all designed to make employee jobs safer, easier, and more productive. Paperwork I fought to get on those machines, via never-ending follow-up e-mails and verbal harangues and end-runs past creeping managerial apathy. And in the end, what has it amounted to?

I walk out of my office at 2:55, buy one last cherry Coke, then take a seat in the deserted upstairs lunchroom to kill some time. I think about what I've learned after fourteen years with The Company, what was gained via that knowledge- and realize I could've done a lot worse. Scores of seminars and college classes- even getting a Bachelor's Degree, not that that made any impact on my manager. But all in all, I learned a lot about others and myself- especially toward the end, when I had to undergo counseling, medication, and cognitive behavior therapy. And while I started out blaming a lot of my troubles on The Company, I eventually learned that sometimes things are out of our control- but that the help we need is found by passing through a portal called Humility, then submitting to all that follows.

And then I think about that letter from the Circuit Court- the one that started it all ...

Wednesday, April 9

THE LETTER ARRIVES EVERY FEW YEARS, and since it's been sent by the State Circuit Court, that can mean only one thing. I open the envelope. Yep. It's a summons, all right. But for some reason, the large boldface words call this a

SPECIAL JURY SUMMONS BY ORDER OF THE PRESIDING JUDGE

> "You are hereby summoned to serve as a juror for a special jury panel. Your service is for one trial, which is estimated to last 3 weeks ..."

Wondering if I've been called to a grand jury, I read the letter again. Then I call the courthouse.

"Well, it's not a grand jury," the person on the other end says. "You'll just have to show up and see."

Turning the summons over in my hands, I wonder- should I even bother? I don't have that much vacation time, and since I'm not a salaried employee, The Company won't reimburse me for time spent at court. I'll have to ask for the standard "Get Out of Jury Duty Free" letter from Human Resources, as I reluctantly did, a couple years before. The HR missive not only covers The Company's corporate ass, but absolves me of guilt or possible harassment by a court clerk, whichever comes first. The only problem with this situation is that- unlike sixty percent of the eligible jurors across our fruited plains (who make it a pastime trying to get out of jury duty)- I *want* to serve.

A couple years earlier I'd sent an impassioned, but anonymous, letter to Mr. Big. I questioned the corporate policy forbidding hourly employees from being reimbursed for serving as jurors. I waited for a month but got no response. Then, at the monthly employee meeting, Mr. Big read my unsigned letter to the troops. I expected some sort of policy change, even a few comments about the importance of serving. Instead, our leader recounted his one experience with jury duty, smirking all the way. Reporting for duty, he'd ended up sitting on his butt the entire day, with nothing to do. Then this captain of industry returned home, reflected on the experience, and concluded that if the justice system was going to waste his valuable time, he'd be damned if he was going to pay any hourly employee to pull R & R at the courthouse, playing pinochle or sleeping or watching TV. Of course, if any of Mr. Big's salaried personnel wanted to serve, he'd pay for it all. His cavalier attitude and misrepresentation of jury service pissed me off.

Reflecting on Mr. Big's non-response to my concerns, I decide that whatever happens, I'll report to the courthouse in three weeks. At least I can see what's going on before I bail on my civic duty. But prior to making that journey, I have to inform Polly. She's not only my boss, but also the resident friendly dictator.

Thursday, April 10

I KNOCK ON THE DOOR and she waves me inside, all smiles. Polly Pot oversees the fifteen employees that constitute the Quality Assurance Department. A slender, middle-aged Vietnamese woman, she's of average height, with long black hair, dark eyes, an abundance of facial paint, and a penchant for wearing her skirts as tight as possible. She sports the pleasant demeanor, is quick to laugh and heap praise. But velvet knife at the ready, she has no compunction about chucking anyone she dislikes under the company bus. Her list of the formerly-employed grows longer by the month.

"Well, Polly, I just received a summons for jury duty."

"Oh- you're *kidding*. Well, don't worry," she reassures me with condescending verbal hand pats and compulsive nodding. "You can get out of it. Just have HR type up a release letter for you."

"But I don't need the letter. I want to serve."

"You do?" she says, cocking her head.

"Polly, it's a civic duty," I say, trying not to radiate self-righteousness. "The trouble is, company policy makes it almost impossible to serve."

"Really?"

"The Employee Manual states that jury duty is a civic responsibility- that we should serve. But unless you're a salaried employee, The Company won't pay a dime of reimbursement money or ..."

As I continue, she's still nodding- and still not getting it. I'm endeavoring to keep my emotions under control- something that's been easier, as of late, due to the Prozac I've been taking.

"... and juries are an important part of our legal system."

My boss's face is a mixture of condescension and misplaced sympathy, as if she's been listening to a mental patient recounting his latest hallucinations.

"You know," she says, "This is very unusual. You're the first person I've known who actually *wants* to do jury duty."

As I trudge back to my office, I'm on a slow boil. Is Polly saying that my attitude is admirable, or that I'm a vigilante? Terminally naive? A judicial extremist? With Polly I can never tell, for she and I are on the shakiest of ground. The trouble began, a year earlier ...

I SAW HER THROUGH THE HALL WINDOW, striding in my direction.

"Good morning, Dan!" Polly crowed as she entered my office without knocking, then stooped forward and began taping a small placard to the inside of the window.

"What are you doing?"

"Oh, this is a sign that everyone will see when they come to your office," she said, nodding excessively as she showed me the paper- a card with my name, title and other bullcrap printed on it. "It will make you look more professional."

More *professional*? Polly was starting to piss me off.

"I don't want it."

"But it will be *good* for you," she said, nodding and smiling and nodding, as my systolic rocketed north of 180.

"I said I don't want it. Who asked you to do this? Rob?" (Rob was our boss.)

"Oh, *no*," she said. "I just took it on myself," and with a satisfied smile, she started to attach the card.

"Get the hell out of here!"

And she did.

But so incensed was I that I followed her out. After telling her a few more things, I returned to my office, slamming the door so hard that objects leaped from the walls to their death. Meanwhile, Polly went straight to HR. Pursuing a pattern of behavior that would soon become her MO, she tried to get me fired. I was "threatening" her. Hostile work environment and all that rot. But

HR never contacted me. Instead, my boss Rob stopped by.

"So, how's your day going, Dan?"

"I feel like shit. Do you know what Polly did?"

"Yes," he nodded, looking as tranquil as I was not. "I heard all about that."

I then proceeded to take an emotional core dump on Rob. A job I'd once loved had turned to crap. Most of my friends were leaving the company; talented, conscientious engineers who were tired of being pushed around and demeaned. My work as a technical writer had been rewarding and made a lot of difference- back in the day. But times were changing. Standard operating procedures were being integrated into automated programs, rendering me an artifact. My job was becoming meaningless. My career path was gone.

"Is there anything I can do?" Rob asked.

Short of having him put out a contract on Polly, there was nothing my boss could do. It was a he-said, she-said situation. Regardless of Polly's execrable behavior, I'd brought this trouble on myself. My coping skills didn't merely suck; they were non-existent.

"No. But there's something I can do. I'm going to seek help with my anger issues."

What I didn't tell him was that self-destructive thoughts had been flitting in and out of my mind over the last few weeks. I'd be on the second-floor mezzanine, looking down, past the protective railing and wondering what would happen if I just leaped over that barrier to land on the concrete, twenty feet below.

"Well..." Rob said- no doubt overwhelmed by my emotion, but satisfied that I'd found a solution. "Sounds like you've got a plan. Take care, and let me know if there's anything I can do." And then he was gone.

In the throes of angry despair, I called a local hospital and was put in touch with a nurse practitioner. She set me up with a licensed clinical social worker. After speaking with me for twenty minutes, the LCW diagnosed me with mixed anxiety and depression. And so began a prescription for SSRIs- first Prozac, then Citalopram. Then came a major blessing: Cognitive Behavior Therapy- a way to learn how to cope with all that crap at work. And for a while, I did become more cognitive of my behavior.

Much to the joy of many, Polly one day announced her imminent departure from The Company. But then Rob quit. Suddenly and inexplicably, Polly was offered his position, and she jumped at the opportunity. And from that moment forward, I was a charter member of Polly Pot's Excrement List. While others grumbled quietly about her passive-aggressive management style, I was more vocal. She called it "insubordination." Having been summoned to the HR Vice President's office several times, I was placed on a short leash known as the Employee Improvement Program, or PIMP, as I liked to call it. Though I displayed outward signs of improvement, I had to take care. If I was caught cracking jokes during one of Polly's interminable department meetings, or refusing to accompany her and the other department slaves to some local kimchee palace for lunch, I'd be seeking employment opportunities elsewhere.

In celebration of the new year, Polly fired a Quality Inspector for playing games on her PC. Then, I and another Quality Department employee were informed we were spending too much time surfing the Net. We had to sign forms admitting we were guilty of the offense, then were sent home on "decision-making leave" for five days, sans pay. Never mind that a lot of the playing was being done during break time, or that high-paid, salaried employees were watching porn online and hadn't been disciplined.

For the next three months I was the model employee-at least on the outside. Internally, I felt like a mental patient at the local laughing academy- a feeling that intensified as my adversarial relationship with Polly continued to deteriorate.

"THE HELL WITH POLLY," I say as I shake it off and retreat to Dick's office. He's the company's sole Quality Engineer, and the only employee I feel comfortable commiserating with about the sorry state of The Company.

"Well, I just received a summons for jury duty."

"Oh, you're *kidding*. Well, don't worry," he reassures me with a verbal hand pat. "You can get out of it. Just have HR type up a release letter for you..."

Tuesday, April 15

WITHIN A DAY OR TWO, I get an e-mail from Blondie Pollyanna, the HR secretary. She has my very own excuse letter ready. I take it back to my office and look over the employee manual- and get pissed off all over again.

> CIRCUIT OF THE STATE OF XXXXX
>
> ATTN: Jury Coordinator
>
> RE: Daniel Hiland
>
> This letter is in reference to the court summons for Daniel Hiland to appear for jury duty. Daniel is an employee of The Company, Inc. Jury duty will create a two-fold problem in his case.
>
> The Company does not reimburse an employee for jury duty. Daniel will not be able to make up the loss of income. Also, the job duties are in the mainstream of our Data Collection Technician II within our Quality Department, and it would be difficult to be without him for a period of time.
>
> We are therefore requesting relief of the summons.
>
> Sincerely
>
> The Company, Inc.

I return to Blondie's office, waving the request.

"What effect will three weeks away from work have on my attendance status?" (The Company doles out financial rewards to employees with stellar attendance.)

"It's no problem," Blondie says. "After *all*, you've got your excuse letter."

"Okay, then," I say, heating up. "Why does this company encourage hourly employees to serve jury duty, yet makes it impossible to do so?"

"Well," Blondie condescends, "I think you'll find that *most* companies these days don't pay for jury duty service."

"The last two companies I worked for did."

"Well, those were *exceptions*."

Defeated by ignorance, I leave HR before I say something that could get me permanent time off.

Over the next few days, I fantasize about serving as a juror. But, nah- I couldn't afford it- though it would be nice to escape from a job that I affectionately refer to as The Hellhole. At least for a few days. But what are my financial options? Seeing none, I decide to go on with life. But not before firing a shot across the corporate bow.

April Letter to the CEO

Dear Stanley:

The following is a statement in the Employee Handbook: "The Company believes that if an employee is called for jury duty, the employee should meet his or her responsibility as a citizen."

It seems that every two to four years I am called to serve as a juror for the County. With the exception of one call, several years ago (which I had to waive, due to financial hardship), I have always responded to the summons. And why? I strongly believe that serving this way in the court system is a civic duty. Our company manual even states as much. Jury service has always constituted one of the pillars of our legal system.

During every period of jury duty, I have been called to serve on many trials, both civil and criminal. It has been a thrilling, informative and sometimes sobering experience- but a real opportunity to serve the community in such a direct way.

Recently I was informed that I am to report for three weeks of special jury service, starting in early May. This will cost me approximately $2,700, out of pocket. I can go to HR and request a waiver, claiming financial hardship- which means that I cannot do my civic duty because I don't make enough money. I have decided, though, that I am going to take out a loan against my 401 K funds and serve anyway. If this is the price I must pay for being a citizen (while Americans are sacrificing their lives for others in Iraq), then so be it.

"My question to you is: "Why does The Company partially reimburse employees for Big Brothers and Big Sisters, as well as Habitat for Humanity involvement, but not jury duty? I realize that the first two are important and worthy endeavors, but is building homes more important than supporting our legal system?

I respectfully request that jury duty service be included under the definition of Paid Community Involvement, as stated in the Employee Handbook. It won't cost The Company that much. After all, I'll be paying the other $2,250.

Thanks for your time.

Respectfully,

Dan Hiland

Documentation Specialist

I receive no response …

Voir Dire

Friday, May 2

I DRESS IN MY BEST WHITE SHIRT, tie, pants and dress shoes. Armed with a few dollars, the Summons, and that "release" letter, I board the #35, which this morning is packed to the gills with humanity. I don't like riding the bus that much; I'd rather be independent and exercise my God-given right to drive. But downtown parking is expensive, assuming you can fight your way through the heavy traffic in a timely manner.

The bus cruises along a suburban street for a half-mile, then drops down by the Southern Pacific rail yards for a stretch, before rising above the ships and crossing a bridge over the river. Dragon boats share the semi-clean waterway with tugs, eels, carp and whatever else is hanging around down there. As we roll into the city center, I'm looking at the trip through a cyclist's eyes. Wouldn't be a bad bike ride, as long as the weather holds.

I pull the cord and disembark, then walk three blocks to the courthouse. The building is just as I remember it-still grey, still archaic, still official looking, yet as popular as ever. The park across the street is waking up squirrels, transients, and assorted commuters astir. I'm a half-hour early, but the line is out the door and onto the sidewalk. Potential jurors, witnesses, off-duty cops, attorneys, journalists, and unindicted criminals are gathered around me. Our group crawls along, then up granite stairsteps to the inner marble-floored landing and the checkpoint. A couple years ago, I could stroll in the front doors without being scrutinized. Now they're taking no chances.

I remove my belt, glasses, pens, wallet and keys, dumping them in a light-gray dog dish. An officer places the dish on a conveyor belt for scanning. I walk through the full body scanner, hoping my pants don't go to half-mast. Not deemed a threat to the public, I'm waved on by a guard. Gathering my stuff, I see at least eight sheriffs clustered near the entrances.

One thing that hasn't changed is the tiny store, straight ahead, next to the central stairway. It's the only place in the building where one can get a cold can of soda, gum, popcorn, or a sandwich, before ascending to more serious locations. The store is run by a middle-aged blind woman. As I buy a sandwich and a Pepsi, I pull out a bill and place it on the counter, wondering how she knows the denomination, and how far down in hell I'd be thrust for deceiving her. Are there really people who'd stoop that low? Reminded of where I'm at, I conclude that there are, and that most of them are in the building at this very moment. There's a tip jar by the left side of her small window that I drop my change into, almost involuntarily. Then I ask where Jury Room 130 is.

I know the drill: sign in, get a white "JUROR" badge to hang around my neck, then find an empty seat amongst the 150- 200 chairs in that long room. There are plenty of empties, so I choose one halfway back, at the end of the row nearest the wall. The chairs are well-padded, and rockers, no less. Settled back to people-watch, I launch into a fried egg, cheese and ham sandwich. Having forgotten to eat before leaving the house, this hits the culinary spot. Since I forgot to take my Prozac, I wonder what will serve to hit that spot.

Twenty minutes pass. Not a lot of conversation amongst us potential jurors, except at the fringes. Most folks are sleeping, reading, texting or playing on their handhelds. I survey the room, estimating that there are one-hundred-seventy of us. How many are here to serve, as opposed to those anxious to present the excuse letter and get the hell out- back to the comfortable, the familiar?

An official introduces himself.

"The court staff is ready to talk to those who need to be excused, due to serious hardship. But that doesn't include those who don't want to be here," he adds, generating scattered laughter from the troops. "The term *hardship*," the official continues, "applies to those without day-care, or people whose employer won't pay for their time off."

So, I *do* have a valid excuse for leaving. The announcement prompts thirty people to quickly form a line heading into the court staff's small office, excuses in hand and/or mind.

Should I join them? After all, I brought the letter from work.

Don't be a fool. Get in line. You can't afford to do this, remember?

But this could be the Big One. A case unlike any other I've served on.

What about your family? The bills? There'll be other chances.

But maybe there won't. And the letter said this is going to be three weeks of service on one trial. It's got to be something big.

In the end, I remain seated. Maybe it's that dedication to civil service I've been evangelizing about. Or merely an excuse to get away from a dead-end job I loathe. Or maybe it's the right thing to do. For now, I'll watch and wait. Besides, what are the chances of me being picked, amidst these scores of candidates? Rooted to my chair, I relax- and to hell with The Company.

The bail-out line moves forward. It's hard not to be judgmental when looking into the faces of those who return from the staff office, free to head through the exit doors to the outside world. Maybe they do have day-care issues, or they fill too vital a role at work.

9:50 a.m. A tee-shirted young lady two rows ahead is writing in some sort of notebook. As I continue to watch, I suddenly feel a kinship to her; she spends her time writing, while others read or do crosswords or text or speak on their cell phones loud enough that we're all part of the conversation. Time passes as I settle further into that plush black chair, much comfier than the hard one I recall sitting on during previous terms of service. These are more like seats you'd find in the better theaters, every part padded, including the armrests. It was a morning like this- only much colder- some years back, when I sat near a big-screen television in the front of this very room. The results of the presidential race were being decided, and word was coming through about who the new president would be: George Bush. But there wasn't much, if any, reaction. More like group resignation.

10:15 a.m. The official reappears. "We're going to call seventy names. If your name is called, please remain in this room until you receive further instructions. Those names not called are released from further service."

A 50% chance. I sit forward. Waiting. Hoping. The first name is pronounced, and the second, and the third. Before the tenth one, my name is called. I feel like I've just won the lottery. The list of names grows, "oohs," "ahhs," or "dammits" voiced by the lucky winners. Upon the reading of the 70th name, scattered cheers burst forth. I can't tell who's happier: the people who get to leave, or the ones who have to stay. After the exodus, the rest of us are handed lengthy questionnaires to fill out, then pass back to the staff. Papers gathered, we're then told about the nature of the case; alleged fraudulent transactions involving investors and financial institutions. It sounds boring, but you never know.

May 2

CIRCUIT COURT OF THE STATE OF XXXXXX

Jurors:

Thank you for your willingness to serve as jurors on this case.

Please report for jury selection at the following date and time ...

Sincerely,

Jane Doe

Judicial Clerk

Wednesday, May 7

10 a.m. I arrive at Room 548, refreshed and ready to go. I've had a decent night's sleep, and I like these banker's hours. The courtroom is a busy place this morning. At the appointed time, someone in charge calls for order.

"Will all potential jurors please find a seat on the gallery benches at the back of the room? Thank you."

The request herds us all into one spot, where the judge and lawyers can watch us- like we're corralled cattle- guaranteeing we won't come in contact with attorneys, officers of the court, defendants, or plaintiffs. Under the continual gaze of most of the people inside the room, the judge presides. We're brought to order.

"I will now read off the names of the jurors. If your name is called, please come up to the juror's box and take your assigned seat. Jurors 1 – 7 will sit in the front row. Numbers 8 – 12 will take their seats in the back. The three alternate jurors will be seated at the far end."

What my chances are of getting picked? Last week it was fifty-fifty, and I made the cut. But today the odds are steeper. The Court is taking only fifteen out of the seventy available: a 22% chance, at best. Things gets tighter as I realize that of the fifteen chosen, I could end up being a lowly alternate. And alternates have it the worst. They're required to be present for the case proceedings, and take notes, and pay attention- but they'll be dismissed, once jury deliberations begin.

Juror #1 is called and makes her way up to a temporarily-assigned seat in the juror's box. Then #2 is summoned, a desultory fellow in his thirties. Potential #3 is a tallish, enthusiastic woman pushing forty.

The suspense is killing me.

Juror #4 is another thirty-something guy, #5 a young Japanese woman who can't be more than twenty. Then my name is called. I can't believe my luck, but show no emotion as I make my way along the gallery aisle, past the crowd of potentials. A quick left, then a right and up three carpeted steps; the juror's box is a scant twelve inches above everyone but the judge and the court reporter. I walk to mid-row and step down to my swivel chair. Though it feels good to be off my feet, I look across the courtroom, where my gaze meets several pairs of intense, roving eyes. Unidentified men and women in fancy suits, some of whom might be lawyers, are analyzing each of us. I return stares, but not for long. They aren't backing down and I don't want to make waves. Potentially hostile jurors find themselves out the door, so I try to make myself invisible, a mere onlooker- as if that will render me immune to the dreaded peremptory challenge. Once we're seated, the judge welcomes us.

"In the matter before us, plaintiffs contend that the defendants are responsible for losses allegedly suffered as a result of investments made in certain portfolio companies. The defendants deny that they bear any responsibility for said investments."

Beyond those words I can't keep up, rendering my notes faulty from the get-go.

"As potential jurors, you will be asked a series of questions by the attorneys. This process is called *voir dire.* Please answer truthfully. If you are subsequently excused, due to a peremptory challenge by one of the attorneys, you will be excused from further involvement in this trial."

When the questions finally begin, they're also directed at potential jurors in the gallery. Upon realizing this, I feel disappointed. Are us box dwellers merely taking up space in these padded chairs? I glance around the room. Everyone is staring at me or one of my fellow lab specimens. It feels like a game, a competition. There are two professionally dressed women in the back corner, by the exit doors. They look at us and talk quietly. One of them consults her clipboard, scribbles something, then looks our way again. Same for the attorneys seated at those long tables. They all have paperwork in front of them, and I know I'm on there somewhere. The way they stare and stare and stare gives me the sense that they're trying to read our minds, verifying or disproving what they see in our questionnaire answers.

Then there's the defendant, sitting on the front gallery bench. He's looking us over, as well. Enigmatic. Expressionless. He-Whose-Name- Has-Not-Yet-Been-Announced. A lot of the jurors don't even know he's present. But I do. I remember his face from past news articles, when he served as head of the state Republican Party. He ran for Governor at one point, but lost- eventually ousted from his RP position for alleged corrupt activities. Mr. X is what I'll call him. He, like many others present, is studying us, on the off chance that he might recognize someone, or not like someone's looks. Maybe he'll ask his attorney to have undesirables excused, without cause.

11 a.m. It's been one hour in the chair. I'm feeling apprehensive as questions parade through my mind. Will my demeanor, or the things I say under questioning, be grounds for my dismissal? What effect will this little adventure have on my financial situation? We're breaking even at home, but we'll need to clean out most of the savings account to pay tithing and pending bills. I may have to cancel the beach trip Carol and I were planning for our 21st wedding anniversary.

The financial bind we're in began the second week of January, when I had to take that five days off without pay. Then there was the $400 we forked over for Carma and Connor's summer camp fees. $300 for my writing class. $100 for Connor's outdoor school. $500 for Carma's traffic ticket. Add to that the regular day-to-day living expenses, and you get the picture. If I'm chosen for this trial, my vacation time at work will evaporate. I'll have to borrow from the 401K funds. Am I sacrificing too much to stand on principal?

At noon we're all excused for lunch.

1:30 p.m. Back to the chair for more voir dire.

2:50 p.m. The attorneys retire to the judge's chambers to discuss the finalized juror selection.

3:25 p.m. We're still waiting for the gang to return from chambers, and my chair seat is getting harder by the minute. I wonder how the court will pull this off, seeing as there are over fifty unselected jurors in the gallery.

4:05 p.m. The bailiff opens the door to the judge's chambers. Then we're all asked to stand as the judge and the lawyers return to the courtroom, after which we're told we can resume our seats.

"Those jurors who've been selected to sit in the jury box- please return to the gallery area," the judge says. "Thank you for your patience."

As we file to the back of the room, I'm distraught. So that's that. I wonder what I said that merits my disqualification. I tried to be so careful with my answers; balanced, objective, devoid of even a scintilla of bias. But the powers-that-be have rendered their decision, and I'm not part of it. All I can do now is stand there and wait, like everyone else.

The name of Juror #1 is called, and it's a different person than her predecessor- now a middle-aged woman who works her way past the throng, and up to the first chair on the left end of the front row. The desultory #2 is announced and travels to his chair. Same for Juror #3, the tall forty-ish woman. Numbers Four and Five are called- the same people who sat to my right, before.

And then my name is called. I feel like shouting it to the rooftops, but restrain myself. I return to the still-warm chair reserved for Juror #6, feeling like the most blessed of men as I settle down into that padded furniture and take ownership. The other jurors are called, several in the back row coming in as replacements for jurors removed due to peremptory challenges. Then the three alternates are called, and they take up residence on the far-right end of the second row. A mixture of sadness and relief shows on the faces of the now-discarded candidates in the gallery. The judge speaks to us.

"You are the official jurors for this case. I want to thank you for your desire to serve. Please report to the Jury Room tomorrow morning, no later than 9 am. And please do not discuss the details of this case with anyone outside the jury room."

Directing his gaze to the crowd in the back, the judge thanks them for participating, then releases them from further obligation as jurors. Looks like I'll need to take out that loan.

The Trial

Day 1

Thursday, May 8

I RUN THE GAUNTLET THROUGH SECURITY, and ascend three flights of stairs. This will be the seventh jury I've sat on in twenty-eight years, thrown into a small group in an even smaller room with total strangers. Our life, for the next few weeks, will consist of time spent in this cramped space, or in the halls during breaks, or in the huge courtroom. The judge will spell out the restrictions on this first day: no talking about the case until deliberations begin; no talking to each other in the courtroom, unless there is a brief recess; no talking within earshot of the lawyers or their clients; avoiding coverage from the newspaper, radio, TV, or Internet articles about the case at hand; no talking to media representatives about the case.

Accordingly, a cloud of paranoia descends, once I put that "JUROR" badge around my neck. I walk the halls, no longer a civilian. I watch who I stand near in the elevator, on the stairs, out on the street, and even on the bus going and coming from home. Lawyers and their clients and possibly the media could be lurking. The badge has a talisman-like power that causes others within or near the courthouse to either shy away from me, or want to draw near, out of curiosity or some less benign reason.

As us jurors first walk through the courthouse during breaks, some of us stick together. But after a while, one discovers that hanging out with other jurors offers no protection or assurance. And it's not like we can talk to each other about aspects of the case that are bugging us. The desire to not look like part of the herd will cause some, like me, to strike out alone. It's easier to get around and away.

While the newbies are clueless, for old jury vets like me, the anxiety can be pronounced. The specter of a mistrial hovers overhead like a judicial Sword of Damocles. One hears stories about the one juror who misbehaved, causing delay or suspension of a trial. "Boy, those jurors really screwed up! Millions of dollars wasted, years of time and effort down the drain. And all because one of those lunkheads screwed up. Ah-hah-hah-hah-hah..." I try to forget these concerns. But the longer the trial goes, and the more complex the verdict is that we'll have to deliberate on, the larger the specter looms.

Locating the entrance marked "JURY ROOM," I push open the heavy, dark, wooden door, of which there are so many in this building. Several jurors are already here, trying to settle in for our shared journey into the unknown. Typical jury quarters: 10' by 4' white oak table dominating the center of the room. Chairs along each side and ends, leaving barely enough room to squeeze by for trips to the bathroom or the exit. Two restrooms, the larger one marked Women, the smaller one for Men. A small gray bookshelf is attached to the concrete wall near the Men's room door, a coat rack and hangers underneath. The shelf holds no books- only a deck of cards, a pencil and an empty, plastic, gold-and-black water jug. There's a 3' by 4' bulletin board on the opposite wall.

Unlike the room in "Twelve Angry Men," there's no smoking here, as evidenced by a wall plaque forbidding such activity. A silver-painted radiator resides below the windows. It looks like it's been there since the Thirties, and I bet it still works. Then there's the coffee maker, whose thankless job it is to brew an endless supply of crappy coffee that everyone bitches and moans about. Nearby sits a jar full of sugar packets, non-dairy creamer containers and white plastic stirring sticks. Alongside is a stack of magazines no one will read or even pick up, during our stay.

The best part of the room is the set of double windows. Tall and wide, they look out and down five stories to the street and the tall trees in the park across the way. The windows used to open, as evidenced by a rusty flagpole holder jutting out from the ledge. Sealing the windows closed sometime in the past must have accomplished several things at once: it's safer; less likely that jurors will jump out of them after one-too-many hours of deliberation; the room's better insulated; and it prevents anyone from being too patriotic by displaying the Flag.

Jurors trickle in over the next hour, all of us sizing each other up. Once the fifteenth juror shows, Marie the bailiff introduces herself, shares a little about procedure, then shuts the heavy wooden entry door and we wait. In a while, Marie comes back to say that the court is ready for us. So out the door and into the hallway we go, single-file. At the door we wait until our bailiff gets the signal that it's time for us to enter. Then we're off to the jury box, everyone searching for their assigned seat- those swiveling leather-upholstered jobs with wooden arm rests that can tip back without warning and knock the tenant off-balance. As I glance around the room, I see that the gang is all here, except the judge. Marie opens a door behind the bench- the only area that sits higher than us jurors- and requests that all rise. The black-robed judge enters, then we're told we can resume sitting. The judge makes a few comments.

There are two prosecuting attorneys present, to our left: one represents a local investor. Him I'll refer to as Galahad. He's known for defending the Boy Scouts of America against everyone out there who's gunning for them. The other lawyer represents a group of Canadian investors. He'll be known as Canada.

To our right are Galahad and Canada's adversaries, the two defense lawyers. Mr. Rueful is representing a company I'll call Accountants "R" Us This is the same company that did such a bang-up job for Enron; their initials are AA. The same company which allegedly discovered years earlier that Mr. X had been poaching investor funds, yet continued working for him because they needed the money. The same company that's currently dealing with scores of pending civil lawsuits. The same company that now exists only as a pile of money surrounded by lawyers.

Seated to Rueful's right is Mr. Eels, the attorney representing Mr. X., and the reason we're all present. Mr. X, is accused of defrauding investors of millions of dollars, with the assistance of Accountants "R" Us. He moved to Florida three years prior to this trial, which surely has nothing whatsoever to do with his attempted avoidance of possible future legal fees or judgments.

Galahad and Canada take the floor to make their respective opening statements. They go into a lot of detail about things of a financial nature, and soon I'm having trouble keeping my eyes open. The only thing that staves off a potentially embarrassing nap is note-taking. I'm scribbling as fast as I can on a 6" by 9" steno pad I've been supplied by the court. By noon break, several things become apparent:

1) Stateside and Canadian investors believe Mr. X and Accountants "R" Us conspired to rip them off for millions of dollars.

2) Mr. X says he did not rip off the investors; he acted in their best interest.

3) Mr. X says that if there's anyone to blame, it's the greedy, lazy investors, the vagaries of the stock market, and Accountants "R" Us, for employing lousy bean counters.

4) Accountants "R" Us believes that it's not their job to "police" their clients; and even if Mr. X did something illegal, they saw no evidence of it.

5) The portrait that Galahad and Canada have painted of Mr. X lands him somewhere in the company of Adolf Hitler and Jack the Ripper.

6) The six pages I've already filled up mean there'd better be more steno pads available.

I go off to lunch bleary-eyed, grateful for the respite. I need time to wake up and prepare for the next round. I think about The Company and start getting angry. Once I return to work, I'm going to request that management remove that "civic duty" phrase from the employee handbook.

I eat a quick lunch and hurry back to the jury room. I don't want to miss anything going on in our new quarters, and showing up late could mean being escorted into the courtroom under a cloud of shame.

Prior to the afternoon session, we start getting to know each other. My fellow jurors include people working in the private and public sectors, the unemployed, and myself- the occupational dead man walking. Stilted conversation becomes relaxed and free-flowing, discussion shifting to the way the attorney's look, their fashion sense (or lack thereof), and personal habits. Someone comments on one lawyer's style of nose-picking. Then there's an expert witness seated with the legal staff who's afflicted with dermatophagia. He sticks a finger into his mouth and starts chewing on it- slowly, then faster. Then it's on to the next digit. Being a lifelong nail biter, I'm no stranger to the milder forms of compulsive self-mutilation. But this future witness takes the cake- or the cuticle, if you will. Sometimes Finger Chewer bites so hard that he grimaces, yet the action continues unabated. It must be the stress. Soon he's inserting a couple digits at a time, before really going at it. The hell of it is that we jurors are the only ones who notice his little performance. During a break, when one of us mentions said mastication to Marie the bailiff, she doesn't know anything about it. What I know is that the more I watch, the more disgusted I become. We're pretty much in agreement that it'll be a cold day in the courtroom before any of us shakes hands with him.

Following Galahad and Canada, the defense attorneys state their clients' contentions. "He'll admit under oath that he borrowed money and that was wrong," confesses Mr. Eels. "He'll tell you it was probably the dumbest thing he's ever done. And make no mistake, he tried to hide it."

I wonder about Mr. X's choice of attorneys. Did he get a discount somewhere? Regardless, I'm pretty sure I don't want Eels defending me if I ever get in legal trouble. I'm also curious about that word "borrowed." If I helped myself to $3,800,000 of someone else's money, never intending to pay it back, maybe I could tell the judge I "borrowed" it. That's not the same thing as stealing, right? And if the judge doesn't buy that excuse, I'm sure I'll be acquitted due to the contrite, self-effacing confession-that I was stupid enough to hide my actions.

And so, the first witness is called to the stand: Money Man, a local multimillionaire and philanthropist. A long-time friend of Mr. X, MM is smiling, pleasant and unassuming. After answering questions about his association with X, Money Man is asked to speak of his own family, whose influence and affluence go back decades. They've donated large portions of their money to the community for medical research, education, art, culture and Jewish causes. As I listen to his credentials and accomplishments, I realize how good of a job his attorney is doing of establishing MM's credibility as a witness.

But the pleasant demeanor turns serious, after the plaintiff attorneys recite a list of instances where Mr. X deceived Money Man over the course of a decade.

"It's a tragedy of Shakespearean proportions," the witness ruefully admits. Then he's asked to tell the court how he felt, upon discovering, only a couple days before the trial, that Mr. X had ripped him off for millions.

"He was best man at my wedding. I treated him like a son!" Money Man shouts, eyes blazing as his fist pounds the podium. At this point he's excused by the attorney. He composes himself and returns to the gallery.

Day 2

Friday, May 9

SUFFERING IN SILENCE is not my strong suit. The Company's jury duty policy continues to piss me off. And I have no reservations about sharing this anger with others. But am I taking it too far? The court officer did tell us, going in, that financial hardship is a valid excuse. So, am I sacrificing part of my retirement money for the sake of a principle? Or is there something else going on here? Like the fact that I despise my boss and the meaningless nature of my job so much that jury duty is a golden opportunity to be absent from work? It's an emotional whipsaw. On the one hand, I'm seeing hypocrisy in The Company's stance on jury duty compensation; they give it half-hearted support, but have no problem shoveling cash at other causes they see as politically acceptable. Then there's me, Joe Citizen, who's telling everyone within earshot about the importance of serving as a juror, all the while complaining about not being compensated.

But it's a new day. Once we're assembled in the JR, Juror Eleven holds up a copy of today's edition of the daily paper's business section. A headline in large, tall letters announces the start of the trial. Without thinking, I ask if I can read it when she's done. I've no sooner made the request than the rest of the crew reminds me that that's not allowed. I'm embarrassed, having already forgotten the judge's warning from the previous day. When Marie the bailiff stops by, collective guilt and an instinct for self-preservation prompt several jurors to tell her about the newspaper in our midst. At Marie's request, Eleven takes the paper with her to the box. Once we're seated, the judge turns to us and offers a stern reminder to not read anything related to the case, after which the bailiff takes the newspaper from Eleven. While all of this is going on, two attorneys are watching Eleven and making comments to each other.

Once the business at hand is commenced, the Defense starts raising objections. It's the accounting firm's turn on the griddle, and Rueful doesn't like it one bit. Galahad introduces CPA Extraordinaire, a recognized expert in the field of accounting and reporting standards. After conducting three hundred hours of research into ten thousand documents, CPA Extraordinaire concluded that Accountants "R" Us purposely ignored its responsibility to its client. He bases this accusation, in part, on the poor condition of the paperwork received from Mr. X's bookkeeper, who apparently "never passed Bookkeeping 101 in high school."

As interesting as all of this must be to the bookkeepers in the audience, my attention wanders. I look around the room. The curtains in the courtroom covering the high windows above and behind us are closed this morning, even though it's overcast outside. Since the court staff has not turned on the lights above the box, I wonder if it's part of some heightened security measures, on the off chance that someone could see inside the courtroom windows from behind the jury. Then I realize I'm being paranoid, and focus again on the trial. But I haven't missed much. The attorneys are still objecting to each other's words. Miscommunication seems to be the order of the day. It gets so contentious that we're asked to go back to the JR.

At 3:30, the judge announces that Finger Chewer will be excused from the trial. He has to leave town and will return at a later date. It's a real break for me, as FC's mastication habits have become a major distraction. I don't need any more of those than I already have.

As the session winds down, the defense attorneys hammer away at one witness's credibility. Sensing a possible opening, they capitalize on his inability to remember certain names, dates and events. It's easy to see what they're trying to accomplish. We recess for the day, at 5 pm. A good thing, too, as information overload is setting in.

Monday, May 12

STRENGTHENED BY THE RESOLVE to continue earning a living, I drive to work and punch in. As I climb stairs to my second-floor office, I feel like a ghost here. Why show up after having been gone for the last three workdays in a row? There are no repercussions, no one clamoring for my help with anything. Feeling unwanted, I'm only going to spend four hours here, then get the hell out. I putter around at my desk, look over some files and a death march project. Then I discover a new email ...

From: Polly Pot

To: Me

CC: VP HR; Blondie Pollyanna

Subject: Jury Duty

Hi: We approved your time-off request for serving jury duty from 5/14 through 5/30. Per your request, we will be using your accrued 31 vacation hours to cover for part of your time off, and the rest will be without pay.

While the Company is supporting your wish to serve the community, we'd like to ask for your support to The Company's needs; that is, coming to work on the day that you are not needed to be in the courtroom or on the day that you are needed to be in the courtroom only half-time.

As you were telling us that you and your family are facing financial hardship for your being off work for jury duty, we would like to provide you options for working B-shift, C-shift, or any modify shifts to help you out. Please let us know.

Thank you.

Signed, Polly Pot

Knowing that the only place I'm really "needed" is in the Courtroom, I fight off the desire to tell my boss to shove it. I instead reply with a non-committal message, then kill time until noon. I can't drive away from the building fast enough.

Day 3

Wednesday, May 14

BACK TO COURT TODAY. Sort of nice to go from work to jury duty, then back to work again. When I tire of one, I can go to the other.

Get to the Room in plenty of time. Have to fend off feelings of anger after listening to several jurors discussing their time off, and how much their employers are shelling out for jury duty, blah, blah, blah. I have to get over this somehow. Backing off on a previous request, I've sent an email to Stanley the CEO, telling him to please ignore my letter: the one in which I'd asked The Company to help me financially. I go on to say that this is a civic duty I'm performing. As such, I consider it a sacrifice worth making, an opportunity to serve my country. It's self-righteous and martyr-ish, but the only way I know to get my point across.

As we file into the courtroom, I notice a number of reporters sitting in the gallery. Things must be heating up. We take two breaks this morning. One for the current witness, who, in response to a question about his medical condition, gets so graphic that he's cut off in mid-sentence by both the questioning lawyer and the judge, whose TMI alarms have gone off. The other respite occurs when Number Three (Question Lady) passes a note to the bailiff. This prompts the judge to dismiss us for five minutes while he speaks with counsel in his chambers. At this rate, the trial should be wrapping up around Christmas. As to questions for the judge, he answers one I submitted earlier, in reference to the newspaper Number Eleven brought to the jury room.

"I can assure you that there's no possibility of a mistrial at this time, since all of you have assured me that you did not read that story in the local newspaper."

Never in my life, including the worst lecture course in college, have I had to record so much information in such a short time- and about accounting and finances, not two of my strong suits. The steno pad the court gave me is already half-full of disparate, arcane information that makes sense only to people like Mr. CPA Extraordinaire, and today's expert witness, the Forensic Accountant. During the course of F.A.'s tortuous journey through ten-thousand of Accountants "R" Us-prepared tax returns, financial statements, and documents called compilation reports, he discovered that said accounting firm had made material misstatements, failed to communicate these to clients, and failed to comply with compilation report standards- making it impossible to identify Mr. X's fraudulent activities.

In order for us uninformed jurors to understand the truly heinous nature of CPA Extraordinaire's conclusions, we're treated to a crash course on the necessary elements of something called "compilation reports." And to understand those, we have to be educated about the "framework for accounting principles," which relies on "presentation" and "disclosure" principles. There's "understanding with the entity," in which "an accountant will inform management of any material errors, and any fraud or illegal acts." In other words, CPAs have fraud-detection responsibility- "fraud" defined as "an intentional act that results in material misstatements in financial statements that are the subject of an audit."

But that's where information overload sets in. Synaptic activities within my brain begin shorting out, overworked axons and dendrites (or whatever the hell they're called) throwing in the low-voltage towel. As my reasoning powers all but shut down, I resort to a fallback position- frenzied note-taking. Types of misstatements are explained, as are compilation service standards. We're told by CPA Extraordinaire that Accountants "R" Us put blinders on when they performed engagements. We're informed that Accountants "R" Us prepared tax returns for Mr. X, knowing they were crap. We're shown Exhibit 778, a transmitted letter proving that their tax preparer knew nothing about accounting standards. We look at balance sheets. We're treated to the sight of a Profit and Loss Comparison Sheet. We're apprised of more balance sheets, check register evidence, another compilation report, more letters, journal entries, another compilation report, general ledger entries, more material misstatements, a Statement of Assets and Liabilities, illegal fund transfers fraudulent financial statements for all three funds, stock certificate lists, more fishy letters asset misappropriation fishy memos fraudulent general ledger entries conflicts of interest not reported by AccountantsR"Usriskalertsandfiduciaryduty...

Sixteen pages of notes later, my brains have turned to mush. Should be a lot of fun trying to analyze this mess later, during deliberations. When lunch time arrives, I'm more than ready.

I'm starting to realize that had I joined the other thirty people who asked to be excused that first day, I would have regretted the decision for the rest of my life. Instead, I'm nursing a grudge against The Company, though unsure how valid my gripe is. I'm not in favor of a state law forcing any business to pay for jury duty, but I wish there was one against hypocrisy.

During a break, I'm sharing information with Number Five about past jury service, cases I've been on, and what deliberations were like. I'm on a roll, the Man of Experience, queuing up stories in my head to share, when Number Three (the Question Lady) interrupts-

"Uh, Dan?"

"Yes?"

"Please stop."

"What? Stop what?"

"Stop discussing all that jury information."

"Why?"

"It's making me uncomfortable."

"What? It has nothing to do with this case. Nothing at all."

"Well, I wish you'd stop."

"You're taking this too seriously." But now I'm pissed.

"*Okay.* From now on I'll shut up about legal stuff and just discuss the weather and NBA games."

That'll show her.

Later on, we head to the courtroom, via the hallway. While waiting in our single file line, I feel a tap on my shoulder. It's Number Three.

"I'm sorry, Dan," she whispers. "I'm only trying to keep the jury out of trouble."

"Well, I have thin skin," I tell her. "I get offended too easily."

So that's the end of that. By her demeanor I can see that she hasn't a mean bone in her body, and means me no offense.

Once we're seated in the jury box, information overload begins anew. If I weren't so fatigued, I'd have worked up no small measure of anger and resentment about the way all this accounting minutiae is being thrown at us. But recess eventually arrives. I exit the courthouse on auto-pilot, walk to the bus stop on impulse power, and return home an empty shell. I have little idea as to what happened during the trial this day, and I don't care.

Day 4

Thursday, May 15

BEFORE LEAVING THE HOUSE, I inadvertently see a headline in the daily paper about one of the players in the trial. Though curious as to the content, I don't have my glasses on and am thus rescued from temptation. But I'd like to read it to gain a clearer understanding of what the hell is going on with the case. For all the notes I've been taking, I still don't have the big picture, unlike the lawyers and reporters, who've been following Mr. X's escapades for years. Accordingly, it's a test of integrity to not read these articles, after promising the court I wouldn't. After all, no one will know, right? Problem is, I still have a conscience, so it doesn't matter who else does or doesn't know, because I do- and that's all that counts. Besides, my poker face has a time limit.

When we arrive in the courtroom for today's festivities, the judge informs us that Alternate Juror #3 has been dismissed for personal reasons. And though alternates only exist to take the place of one of us "official" jurors- in case of illness, disqualification, etc.- she and the other two have been diligent record-keepers, just as involved and observant as the rest of us. I feel sorry for the Three, for once the closing arguments are made, and the judge instructs the jury about the charges being made, and we head off to the jury room to deliberate, the alternates will be thanked for their service, then excused from the case.

Plaintiff's expert witness, Forensic Accountant, again takes the stand, and is questioned by Galahad and Canada. FA was hired five years ago to scour electronic records for proof that Mr. X stole money from the investors. He spent 285 hours (at seven hours a day) poring over fourteen years' worth of records. While what he found in the records was troubling, the fact that Mr. X and his associates were not supplying other needed records- even after months of requests- was equally bothersome; it's the type of behavior one would expect from a person with something to hide. QuickBooks had to be searched for the needed information.

Then the defense attorneys begin their examination of the witness. FA tells them that he represents the investors committee, which may suggest bias against Mr. X. A few questions are asked in an attempt to impeach the witness, but his credibility survives these subtle and not so subtle attacks. Yet the lawyers continue.

"Are you a CPA?"

"No, I am not. I'm a forensic accountant."

Eventually the defense gives up and Galahad conducts a re-direct. The witness answers questions about some draft and final reports, and says that as late as eight months after he was hired by the investors committee, he didn't know that Accountants "R" Us was handling the accounting for Mr. X. Forensic Accountant describes the monumental task involved in searching for info in the

QuickBooks database, due to its size. Not knowing what he was looking for didn't help matters. The witness is then excused.

Money Man takes the stand, and is cross-examined by the defense.

"Yes, Mr. X did supply me with some business-related information, which represented a degree of due diligence."

"Yes, I did receive a letter detailing the assignment of 20,000 shares of stock" (inferring that Mr. X was not being deceptive, due to his proactive delivery of the information to Money Man).

But when defense asks Money Man how Mr. X was going to pay him back, M.M. gets pissed off at the lawyer-which is when the judge calls the attorneys to his chambers. At this point, screeching feedback begins emanating from one of the microphones, causing some tense moments for a technician.

Technical and legal issues resolved, Money Man is cross-examined a bit more, then Galahad does a re-direct.

"Yes, Mr. X did send me a check for $250,000."

"No, Mr. X neglected to say where the money came from."

Galahad having cast enough doubt on Mr. X to re-establish his crappy reputation, recess is called for the rest of the day.

Day 5

Friday, May 16

HOTTEST DAY OF THE YEAR- in the mid-nineties. Looking out back, I discover that most of the Gang of Seven- our collection of rabbits- have escaped from their cage. Carol and I chase them down and put them back in jail. They've been having fun, all wet fur and muddy paws. Wiping my shoes, pants and hands of mud and rabbit fur, I run for the bus.

Another mind-numbing morning of testimony about financial minutiae: tax engagement letters, the procedural aspects of return preparation, obligation to exercise due diligence, limited liability agreements, Exhibit #1022, Exhibit #777, Exhibit #778, Exhibit #779, and balance sheets. Though some of it is interesting, much time is wasted by Galahad trying to get a stunningly pretty CPA witness to remember important details surrounding her part in tax report preparations- reports that could prove Mr. X's complicity in fraudulent transactions. Then, Exhibit 1022 (an amended and restated operating agreement); check registers from Mr. X to the current witness; Exhibit 1253; Exhibit 1269 ...

My mind drifts off, away from the courtroom, down the stone stair-steps and out the door to the busy street-then I'm across the river, back to my house and those silly rabbits ...

Three weeks before the trial began, I'd come home from work, and noticed Emily, our black-and-white, in-house, small critter exterminating cat, parked behind Bud's cage. She was transfixed, as only a cat in hunting mode can be, by something I couldn't see. Bud had dug a hole near the edge of his cage, a week earlier, then filled it up again. It turned out to be a tunnel extending a foot past the edge of the cage base. It had collapsed. I'd placed some flat blocks over the top of the hole, so Bud wouldn't escape, and to prevent any of us from getting broken ankles. Now there was a two-inch gap through which Emily was presently shoving her paws. I moved in for a closer look. The cat looked up at me: *You're interfering with my business. Would you please leave?*

My mind flashed back to the two dead baby bunnies I'd discovered in the yard a few days before. One of the partially-eaten corpses had been drug into the garage, a trophy kill from Emily. The other was found a few feet from Bud's cage. Chasing the cat away, I kneeled and pulled the flat blocks apart. Looking down into the gloom, I spotted movement. Just as I thought: mice! They were too small to be rats. Ready to relinquish my spot to the cat- who was sitting impatiently nearby- I noticed that the activity below was increasing. Whatever it was seemed larger than any mice I'd ever seen. Pulling the blocks aside, I saw a flash of brown. It was a baby rabbit. I looked closer. Now I saw two baby rabbits. So that was where the dead bunnies had come from. Carol came out and helped me drag Bud's cage away from the hole. Then she shined a flashlight down as I stuck my trembling hand into the void, fully expecting to get bit by a protective momma bunny. Instead, all I felt were several warm, furry bodies. In a new twist on the magician pulling rabbits out of a hat, I brought one out and placed it in a plastic tub. It was a beautiful, light-brown baby rabbit. I pulled out another. Then another. Then another, no sign of Momma in the process. All told, there were seven of the critters. I felt sort of giddy looking at all of those cute little buggers. On the one hand, I was excited about holding and playing with baby rabbits, as it was the first time I'd ever seen them this young. On the other, I wondered what we'd do with them all. We carried the tub inside and placed it on the kitchen table. They were indeed beautiful creatures, all sandy brown. The same color as Bud. So, where had they come from? Who were the parents? How had they gotten into that hole? Three of our five adult rabbits were white. Nibbles, the lop, was black and white. Which left Bud.

Bud was a Flemish Giant- one of the biggest breeds there are. Bud was also a boy. At least that's what the lady at the rabbitry told us the previous summer when we'd bought him. And she was an expert. She'd shown us her storage room, two of the walls covered with pink and red and yellow and blue ribbons from all the shows she'd placed at. After paying the woman, we'd gotten Bud into the front seat of the truck, where my son held him all the way home. I don't know who was happier- my son or the rabbit.

Baby rabbits secure, I brought Bud inside and sat down in the swiveling office chair. With the furry beast stretched along my chest diagonally, from shoulder to hip, I felt around on his belly. And there they were- two short rows of evenly spaced teats. Suspicions were confirmed a bit later, when the Gang of Seven dove under Bud's belly in a frenzied attempt to get milk. The reason we never saw this behavior before was that baby bunnies only get five minutes a day for nursing, before Mom closes the Milk Bar. Bud would uncover the hole she'd dug, go below to feed the troops, then run upstairs and cover the hole again. No wonder we never had a clue.

The attorney gets a few more "I don't remember" answers from the CPA goddess, who is then excused from further testimony. Then the judge excuses us for the blessed noon break.

At lunchtime I write some crappy poetry:

LUNCHTIME IN THE CITY CAFÉ

Sunlit blossoms drifting down around the park trees and people, like slow-motion snowflakes.

Reluctant snowflakes that are okay with the trip,

But not the destination-

But at least the end is quick for the flakes.

Whereas blossoms will be stepped on

And kicked around

And blown sideways,

Looking like snow

Until one peers closer and sees the yellowing of the blossoms.

Their time and purpose now past

As the cells break down

And shrivel,

Drying up to a tissue-like nothingness.

Back to court.

Question Lady is again peppering the judge with queries, the latest set forcing him to fire a return shot across our collective bow. No, we are not to discuss the case or its various components, such as the attorneys, witnesses, etc. Then a recess is called, for some reason, so it's back to the jury room.

Off scatter most of the jurors for a smoke break or to stretch their legs. I pace the polished floor, then gaze out the thick plate glass. Looking down to the street, it doesn't seem that far. But it is. I imagine what it'd be like to jump from the window ledge, five stories up- not being suicidal, but maybe to escape from a fire, or a bad guy, or just out of curiosity. There are two trees, one to each side of the window, though on the other edge of the sidewalk. At first glance, it appears too much of a leap to even reach the branches. So, for purposes of discussion, let's say I don't need to take a running leap. The shallow four-foot-wide ledge wouldn't allow me to, anyway. So, I go for the tree on my right. I have to make a well-calculated jump, aiming for the top and center of the tree, where the branches are the softest. Since I don't want to hit the trunk, I've got to aim for one side or the other.

Let's say I've taken the initiative and jumped. What now? Well, the cannonball isn't an option. I have to hit the vegetation with arms outstretched, but eyes squinted and almost closed. Don't want to poke one out while I'm looking for the perfect bundle of branches. As I hit the limbs, my clothes are being torn up and there's lots of fast snapping and crashing. At this point, one of several possibilities exists:

1) I grab one of the large limbs, which slows me down, but which, at some point, snaps under the strain, slapping me sideways into the trunk.

2) I pass through all the vegetation like a hot knife through butter, and splat on the sidewalk, or if I'm lucky, get hit by a bus. At least that would be quicker.

3) I grab just the right number of branches and fall to the pavement, suffering a lot of bruises and maybe a broken bone or two- but at least I'm still alive.

4) I land square-on, and am unceremoniously impaled by a limb. End of story.

5) I get stuck in the tree, wedged good and tight between two large trunks. But at least I can climb down from there.

6) I pass out on the way to the tree, which would be very unfortunate.

7) I bounce off the tree, which would also be very unfortunate.

We return to court after lunch, ready to go at it- until someone notices an empty chair in the second row. Marie the bailiff runs down the hall to the jury room, then reappears with the errant juror and escorts her to her seat. After the next break, Number Seven comes running in, after awakening from a nap and noticing that the jury room was empty.

Galahad begins questioning Accountants "R" Us CPA Witness #2. Like Witness #1, this CPA has memory problems. He gets testy with the attorney when asked about three fishy-sounding memos, but begrudgingly answers the questions. Yet, when presented with a final memo he wrote, he doesn't recall why he penned it. Galahad is clearly fed up with the obfuscation. He presents Mr. Memory with several memos, one of which is from a subordinate who is questioning an egregious "lack of documentation." Suddenly, this CPA's memory improves. But it's too little and too late for me. Fed up with his crappy attitude and abysmal powers of recall, I've been tallying every "I don't remember." I lose track after thirty.

Accountants "R" Us CPA Witness #3 is next up. Though occasionally reticent with his answers, he proves to be a treasure trove of information. I can see why Galahad saved this man's testimony for the end of the day.

Despite the bonhomie of the previous witness, none of the CPA's questioned today day have admitted that they saw anything improper in Mr. X's paperwork or transactions.

Day 6

Monday, May 19

ANOTHER BEAUTIFUL, SUNNY SPRING MORNING as I stand here at the bus stop- one of those with no shelter overhead, no place to sit except for a large planter area full of ivy, the wooden pilings too covered with plant life for you to know what you are sitting on, should you make the attempt. It's a strange feeling to go to jury duty every work day, as if it were a real job, while the one at The Company languishes. My real job is now a place to go when I don't have anything better to do.

We're getting into a routine. A lot of us show up early so as to not be the person who's holding up the proceedings. But there always seems to be one individual still in the bathroom, or stuck in traffic, or asleep. Makes me wonder if we'll lose another juror before the next two weeks are done.

Once notified it's time to start, we follow the bailiff through the outer hallway. From there we walk single file into the courtroom, where everyone from newspaper reporters and gallery denizens, to the witnesses and legal staff are standing, whether out of respect or tradition I cannot tell. I make my way past them and try to avoid eye contact. Then it's up a couple of steps to the jury box, where us front row dwellers struggle to squeeze past the perpetually swiveling chairs to our assigned seats. After the judge enters and is seated, we all follow suit.

I spend the morning listening to Canada elicit testimony from a CEO/CIO representing the Canadian investor group. Administered by the government, $10,000,000 of investor money was sunk into two funds managed by Mr. X. Less than two years later, Mr. X was screwing around with the funds. The investor group was getting suspicious, though without evidence yet of wrongdoing by Mr. X.

Number Five, to my right, is yawning every two minutes, when she's not nodding off. Suddenly she does a quick, herky-jerky, panicked recovery after leaning back too far in her spring-loaded chair. Now she has no trouble keeping her eyes open. After today's morning break, I nearly do a header over my chair and the low wall, drawing an amused look from the statuesque, ever-typing court reporter.

Defense attorneys question a witness, intent on showing that Mr. X was doing his job properly, and that the investor group had only itself to blame for future investment failures.

We break for lunch at noon. I make a beeline for the City Café, where I order a Coke and cheeseburger surrounded by a plate of greasy fries. This is a good place to sit and write in my green composition book- a thin volume that's become my constant companion. The restaurant is a pleasant place to sit, with plenty of kitchen-generated aromas to savor. Never more than half-full or empty, the café does a steady business, and the food is good. I can look out a 3' by 3' window at the park block, where a combination of working folk and street people peacefully coexist, at least from noon to one. It could be argued that the people lying on sleeping bags are just regular folk out for a day in the sun- but amidst all that dog glitch and spit-infested turf? And with backpacks? I'm pretty sure they're urban vagabonds.

One tall fellow in cutoffs and a tee shirt sticks out. Of all the people in this block, he's the only one who can't stand still. In fact, the only thing Mr. Shaky could be accused of doing consistently is standing, while he shuffles from one foot to the other, arms up, then down, then all around, his body breaking into a few quick dance steps, then stopping as he carries on an intermittent conversation with someone lying on a sleeping bag. Mr. S tosses a wrapper or something on the other person before struggling to don his backpack and fiddle around with the snaps, dancing again from one foot to the other as if something internal were controlling him, driving him on to anything but rest.

The more I watch, the more fidgety and irritable I get. Then, as if to give me and everyone else within view a break, Mr. Shaky goes out of his way to ride one circle around the people he's been talking to, then heads down the sidewalk to the intersection. So much for that guy, I say as I finish my burger and dripping fries. Then I see movement near the bottom of the window. There he is again, talking to a mulletted thirty-something. A cap-backwards graduate of the streets, his companion is a woman with limp, gray hair. Her burning cigarette smoke matches the grayish hue of her skin, while adding a couple decades to her looks. As the threesome talk, Cap Guy stares down the street as if he's watching someone, or for someone, then tosses his empty pop bottle on a small patch of grass at the base of a tree. The woman gives Mr. Shaky her vital stats on a piece of paper, then tosses her half-smoked cig on the ground, signaling an end to the party. Mr. Shaky then heads north, the other two south.

Afternoon questioning by Galahad of the Accountants "R" Us bean counter is damned boring, not to mention irritating, the witness afflicted with chronic memory loss. Galahad presents the accountant with ten separate exhibits of evidence, to which this CPA's number of "I don't remembers" rivals that of last Friday's witness, who oddly enough was a subordinate of today's forgetful one. I can't tell if this fellow is hostile toward Galahad, or truly suffers from bad recall, but he sure is frustrating to watch and listen to. In the end, the attorney pries this out of the man: "Yes, the wording in a particular piece of evidence was a mistake." It's a tacit admission of guilt, as touching upon the question of whether or not Accountants "R" Us screwed up.

At 5 pm we follow Marie the bailiff out of the courtroom, down the hallway and into jury chambers, where we gather our stuff and head for home, most of us by bus or light rail. Short of change, I have to find an ATM and get a twenty out of savings so I can buy a $2.50 ice cream cone, thus getting the $1.75 in change I need for the #35. Never have been a big fan of public transit, but I have to admit that the bus has come in very handy these last couple weeks.

I drop by The Company during the evening hours, thinking I'll put in two or three hours, but after sixty minutes I've had enough and return home. The place sucks wind like there's no tomorrow, yet I depend on it for a paycheck. I've gotten a few responses to job searches on the Internet, but only the last couple have seemed even remotely interesting. And every day I ride the bus to the courthouse. And every day I wonder whether I made the right decision to serve. And every day I wonder what will be the result of all of this.

Day 7

Tuesday, May 20

FINALLY COOLED OFF. It's raining this morning, and time for another round of "Catch the Muddy, Waterlogged Rabbits." They may be cute, but they also know how to make a hell of a mess.

I've brought a Scrabble board to the JR, and started a game with Number One, who's proving to be a formidable opponent.

The morning session is pretty lame: the CPA with the bad memory is being questioned by defense attorney Rueful, and now seems to remember things a lot better. Funny how that works. Said CPA was supposedly encouraging Mr. X to improve the quality of the work his accountant was doing. Mr. X's solution was to replace his current accountant with one from Accountants "R" Us-sort of like changing your drink of choice from rotgut whiskey to low octane gasoline.

Things get more interesting when Galahad cross-examines the CPA. At one point, the attorney observes that the CPAs memory seems to have improved since yesterday. As questioning progresses, the witness starts acting a little spooked, and admits that Accountants "R" Us should have been a little more accurate. Or clear. Or thorough. Canada makes a similar dig about the CPA's improved memory, and it's taking a toll on the witness. There's still a sense that this accountant holds plaintiffs' lawyers in contempt, but he seems less willing to crack jokes at the expense of his interrogators. Showing a clip from the CPAs deposition doesn't do much for his confidence. From what I've seen of the CPAs from Accountants "R" Us, they're all arrogant, condescending, and curiously aloof.

Stepping outside, I pull in a lungful of moist air. The overnight rain has cooled off everything and watered the plants. The air is fresher and the sun is out. And despite the fact that I'm not bringing in enough money to feed my family right now, it's nice to be away from work.

Next on the griddle is another Accountants "R" Us CPA. She explains to the defense attorney that she reported directly to the memory-challenged witness (from earlier in the day). Nine exhibits are shown to her and the court, her initials on most of them. She states that she never suspected anything was amiss with her superiors' attitude toward Mr. X and his way of doing business. Galahad then cross-examines her, beginning with her verification of a $1,737,000 loan of investor money to Mr. X that's listed in the QuickBooks files. Then he asks her to explain emails showing concern about incomplete documentation, information missing from Accountants "R" Us files, and a balance sheet that shows a positive and negative entry for the same transaction amount. Concerning this strange entry, the witness states that Mr. X's accountant "couldn't have done that," and that she was "weak." The question of who did make the entry is not answered.

Canada now steps up to the plate for a brief cross-examination. He asks the CPA to explain how or why record of the aforementioned $1,737,000 loan of investor money to Mr. X does not appear in any of the finalized financial paperwork. He asks about an "adjustment" made for $1,737,000 that changed its classification from a "loan" to something else. The CPA has no answer for the court, and is then excused.

Canada calls to the stand a former portfolio manager for the Canadian investment firm. He testifies that at some point after Canadian investors' funds were placed in Mr. X's hands, communications broke down between the two parties- especially when the investors sought to find out what had happened to their money. The witness also states that Accountants "R" Us was involved in some of the compilations related to the Canadian money. He testifies that an operating agreement between the two parties was amended at some point. At this point, the judge calls for a recess until the following day.

Day 8

Wednesday, May 21

HAD TROUBLE SLEEPING. Got to the courthouse on time, but wasn't able to keep my eyes open during the first ninety minutes of Canada's questioning. Yesterday's Canadian witness verifies the validity of some exhibits he's shown; they document Mr. X's false promises to provide financial statements to the Canadian investment firm. The delaying tactics bought Mr. X months of time to cover his ass, as he moved fund money from one shell to another, paying off creditors, or pocketing some of the money, or both.

When the witness examined the operating agreement entered into by the Canadians and Mr. X, he told the investment firm that the loans should never have been made to Mr. X in the first place. He further advised the firm to request repayment of the money from Mr. X immediately. Despite reassurances from the latter (over a period of months), that the money would be paid back-and despite supposed documents showing this to be true-the witness discovered that only part of the funds had been repaid. From there on, Mr. X was involved in a complex set of maneuvers that hid his theft of investor funds: operating agreement violations, delaying tactics, and falsification of financial records.

By this time, Mr. X's guilt is a foregone conclusion, as far as I'm concerned. What remains to be seen is the extent of his damage to the investors' funds, and how complicit Accountants "R" Us is in this growing nightmare.

After a short nap in the JR, things get better. Having the attorneys barking at each other helps, as well. It's funny how they can be so very polite to one another, until one of them says something the other doesn't like. Then out come the fangs and knives.

The restaurant window I'm looking out of takes in the main intersection, uniformed officers meeting there to head for lunch, court appointments or patrols. A photographer a half-block east has been circling a fountain in the middle of the street, snapping shots of the large elk statue. I've seen this landmark many times, but I've never stopped to ask why someone would erect a monument to an elk. Though wine country is nearby, I know this is not homage to that fraternal drinking order, the Elks Club. And no elk ever saved anyone's life. And the animal is not a statesman, which is not to say that a full-grown elk couldn't do as good a job of legislating as some of the specimens we have at the State Capitol. Might have trouble getting that rack of antlers through the front door, but accommodations could be made. Oh, well. It could be worse; the city fathers could have erected a likeness of Stalin or Lenin. The guy is still taking pictures. He must really like elk. Then again, maybe he thinks it's alive.

With the court day waning, I'm falling asleep every two minutes. Galahad calls another Accountants "R" Us

CPA to the stand, but before he can get very far into the subject matter at hand, the judge calls for a recess at 4:50. Soon I'm on the bus, headed for writing class.

Day 9

May 22

CIRCUIT COURT OF THE STATE OF XXXXXXX

To Whom it May Concern:

Since Wednesday, May 7, Daniel Hiland has been serving as juror in a civil trial at the County Courthouse. His presence is required at the Courthouse from 8:00 a.m. until 5:00 p.m. daily. Current estimates by the Court indicate that the trial will last through Friday, June 6. Jurors may be required to serve longer depending on the needs of the Court.

Please excuse Mr. Hiland's absence from work throughout the duration of the trial.

Please contact our court if you have any questions regarding jury service.

Sincerely,

Marie ---------

Judicial Clerk for Judge ---------

GALAHAD CONTINUES HIS QUESTIONING of yesterday's final witness. Another Accountants "R" Us CPA, this witness isn't interested in arguing, but he's still adverse. He answers many questions concerning his meetings with Mr. X, as well as correspondence that was flying back and forth between Mr. X and Accountants "R" Us representatives. As a result of the witness's exposure to all this information, he began to suspect that something was wrong with some of the transactions taking place, but hesitated to notify his superiors or associates related to Mr. X's actions. Ways were being found to cover up Mr. X's travel and expenses, and transfer them to the funds manager. Records of where investor funds were going were vague: was Mr. X using them to purchase stock, or was the money going to his personal account? The witness had more meetings with Mr. X. Evidence surfaced showing that travel and expenses incurred by Mr. X- to the tune of $20,000- were being listed as if they were capital expenses. During questioning, Galahad is told that much of the documentation being discussed is being stored in this CPAs garage.

Canada takes over, asking questions about the funds, as well as audits that were to be performed. The witness verifies existence of a letter showing that a loan of $3,628,000 was transferred from the investor funds directly to Mr. X. He even admits to personal knowledge of the nature of the loan, but doesn't inform others who should be made aware. More damning is this witness's acknowledgment of a letter from an associate requesting that they "keep quiet" about a particular transaction, to protect Mr. X's reputation and his accounts. Accordingly, the CPA kept quiet, not even letting the biggest investor know of the cover-up. In essence, Galahad and Canada have gotten this CPA to admit that there was a lack of due diligence on the part of Accountants "R" Us, in relation to its clients.

After lunch, plaintiffs call an investor who lost $125,000 to Mr. X. It's the same sad story: investor gave money to Mr. X, who then did something with the funds for which they weren't intended. When the investor asked for the promised return of said funds, delaying tactics were employed. Again. And Again. And again. Sometimes, Mr. X paid some or all of the funds back, but with money he procured from some other poor sap of an investor. The process has "Ponzi" written all over it.

Then the session turns ugly, as the current witness disagrees with a defense attorney during cross-examination. When Canada questions said witness, Rueful and Eels start giggling, the sound of which can be heard all over the courtroom. Mr. Galahad turns and stares at the chucklers. He is not laughing. As court recesses for the day, Galahad asks if he can speak with the judge, off the record.

Went to work this evening, for a couple of hours. The more I go in to do catch-up work, the less I want to be there- and the less the job seems to mean. Once again, I feel like the Company ghost: been there for many years and seen it all. And the longer I stay, the more transparent I become- as in, "Ah, he's never going to quit. He's too important. Besides, he doesn't make that much; he can't afford to quit." Well, I've finally arrived at a point where I couldn't care less if they let me go. I have no idea where a new job will come from, but at least some of the pressure is gone.

Day 10

Friday, May 23

ANOTHER GLORIOUS, RAINY JURY DAY. I'm standing at a different bus stop than normal. Short of change, I have to break a twenty at the local Plaid to get the $1.75 needed for the bus. Been thinking about all those stories I've written, none of which have been revised. I'm still not enough of a convert to the revision process to overcome the inertia of procrastination. Maybe I could hire someone to point a loaded revolver at me until I start revising the first draft…

I take a walk around the fifth floor this morning, as the JR isn't open yet. Count seven JRs, maybe more, as a couple doors are unmarked. You never know, around this place. There are judge's chambers, rooms for judicial assistants, and rest rooms. There are ninety-eight steps from the first floor to the fifth; white granite steps, some of which have been trod on so much that they have dips worn into them, concaved from millions of shoes: lawyers, judges, parole officers, police, jurors, court reporters, bailiffs, photographers, newspaper reporters, and janitors.

Once the JR opens, I enter and notice that some blessed soul has brought a bunch of donuts, others arriving with cookies, so we've got enough junk food to last us the rest of the day. We're supposed to be released early, according to the judge.

After lunch we get an unplanned break, while the sound system goes haywire. I get in part of a Scrabble game before we're called back in. We hear testimony about how screwed up the defendant's records are. We listen to Accountant Stoneface (a witness for the plaintiff) go on and on about the documents. At one point he provides some unintended comic relief while trying to explain the significance of a two-page letter (known as the Five Hats memo), which is displayed on a projector screen. The second page shows five signatures for approval, all of them belonging to Mr. X. I see that and start giggling. No wonder someone might think the signer was crooked. Mr. X was signing over other people's money to himself, and with his own permission. As I muse on this, the first page is again displayed.

"So, who was this letter sent to?" Galahad asks.

"It was for the signer only," Stoneface says.

"And what was he doing?"

"Explaining it to himself."

I'm looking at my shoes, trying to suppress mirth about the ludicrous nature of X's behavior. It doesn't help that Canada, sitting across the room, is suppressing a grin while Stoneface struggles with three full binders, banging the microphone first with one, then another. Even the judge is amused. Thankfully, court recesses before I lose it. It'll be nice to have three days off.

Day 11

Tuesday, May 27

WAKE UP, LISTEN TO THE RADIO for a couple minutes, take a shower, take a Prozac, get dressed, brush hair and teeth, put on socks and shoes, glance at the paper, find juror tag and glasses and wallet and $1.75 change for the bus, grab pens and notebook, and I'm ready to go. I barely make it to the bus on time. This is the most I've ever ridden the bus. I make the observation in my journal that there's not much difference between city transportation and a sanitation truck, the main one being that the bus drops off as much as it picks up.

Get settled in at the jury room and finish a game of Scrabble with one of the ladies. Get my butt kicked, but we start another and things are looking much better.

This morning the gallery population is up to fourteen. It's the largest crowd we've had yet, if you don't count the groups of school kids that come and go with the regularity of a revolving door.

Most mornings it takes me fifteen minutes to mentally get into gear enough that I can follow the proceedings. But there's no problem today. The defense is questioning a plaintiff witness who doesn't take kindly to trick questions or his credibility being dismissed. While not sleepy, the juror to my right gets bored easily, showing it with restless movements and dismissive yawns which return every thirty seconds. Her apathy is irritating.

Lunchtime at the restaurant. There's a lady leaning against the bicycle hitching post outside. An open book cradled in one hand, cigarette in the other, she reads while taking a puff, then exhales, then puffs and releases. The way she's multitasking makes me wonder if the smoking routine is on auto-pilot. At some point- say, if the book becomes too interesting- she might slip up and stick the lit end in her mouth. Or start her clothing on fire. Or accidentally burn a passerby. Since she smokes, not with each breath but every two or three, how does she stay focused on what she's reading? I couldn't stand the interruptions. Well, she just switched hands.

This afternoon a key witness for the plaintiff has taken the stand. There are nineteen spectators in the gallery, a sign that things are heating up. I can hardly wait to see how crowded the courtroom is by week's end. Other data is being tracked, as well. Some of the female jurors are taking note of the ties worn by the attorneys, judging them for taste or lack thereof, color, and who knows what else. They're no longer rating hair styles (at least for those who still have their own hair), nose-picking techniques and habits no longer a source of fascination or conjecture. Regardless, we're awaiting the return of the Hand Chewer, whose reappearance on the stand has been sadly delayed.

Day 12

Wednesday, May 28

SITTING AT THE BUS STOP, WAITING.

Waiting for the bus to come.

Waiting for a better job to come.

Waiting for THAT opportunity to come up to me, panting, then fall into my lap saying "Oh- thank goodness I've finally found you."

I think I'm done waiting.

One of the things that risk-taking does is open one's mind to taking more risks. I'm considering giving notice at work- that I'll be leaving in thirty days. But what would that accomplish? It would force me to look for another job. It would free up my 401K money. It would help me see that I can take risks and survive the consequences. I've been looking for a way out of The Company. Maybe this interruption of my work is a blessing in disguise, much as layoffs in the past got me unstuck from other occupational ruts I was in. Wouldn't it make for a less regret-filled existence to know that I took charge of my life at some point- made some sort of change, did something I could look back on someday and say, "That's the day I really started living." Of course, on the other side of all this brave talk stands that ogre, Money- enough to be able to feed my family, pay the bills, and not lose our home.

I probably won't quit my job just yet, but one thing is certain: I need to get serious about writing. I've got to write more, watch TV less. I've got to start revising the hell out of the best stuff. I've got to start submitting stuff. I need to get the zine thing going.

As far as legal matters go, plaintiff's attorneys have finally called Mr. X, the man who'll be the focus of intensive questioning by both sides. Soon we recess. I step outside for some fresh, unadjudicated air. It's cold and grey, threatening to rain; feels more like March than the butt end of May. I wonder what's going on at home, what's going on anywhere else in the real world. People are walking, riding, driving here and there on the streets that surround the courthouse, oblivious to what's happening here in the courtroom I now inhabit. Then it's time to ascend to the fifth floor.

Two attorneys take turns raking Mr. X over the legal coals until court recesses for the day.

Writing class is this evening, and for a moment I consider dropping it. Then I dismiss the idea as another attempt to flee commitment. Either that or I'm just burned out on the course.

Day 13

Thursday, May 29

ONE WAY TO SPLIT THE ATOM.
Two ways to split my personality.
Five ways to split the paycheck.
One-thousand ways to split hairs.

10:30 a.m. Number Five is AWOL. Word is she stayed overnight at her boyfriend's house and then overslept. The only good part of this is that we've had time to finish a three-way Scrabble game.

11:15 a.m. Marie the bailiff sent us off on an extended break- until 1:30 pm. Number Five's little mistake has cost me four hour's wages. And yes, I'm pissed.

I step out for a bite to eat, then return to the jury room. Marie stops by and asks me to let her know when Number Five shows up. She wants to have a little talk with the missing juror; so do some of us and the judge.

I have all this time. I can write anything I want, but when I sit down at the big jury table with an hour all to myself, the mind goes not blank but "Yecchh!" I don't think it's burnout so much as laziness. I was reading a book last night and came across an interesting idea: write a book in thirty days. It works out to eight pages daily. I think I could do that many in a day, all right, but what would it be like to repeat that every single day, for a month? I imagine that one would be a better writer, as a result. The hard part- or one of several hard parts- would be finding the time and the place, not to mention the content. I guess I could write at work, or once I get home ...

11:45 a.m. Number Five finally makes her appearance. I waste no time telling her how much her tardiness has cost me. She apologizes and much of my anger melts away. My only hope is that she's learned something from this, because it's affected a large number of people.

A Proclamation

Be it known that on this day, during the noon hour of jury duty, I, Dan Hiland, being of questionable mind and impulsive nature, did begin a special writing project. Said project will extend from today until June 28th, at which time I will have completed something never attempted by this human before: to wit, approximately 248 pages filled with the good and the bad, the menial and the profound, the beautiful and the gauche. Said project will require due diligence (as they are so fond of saying, here in the halls of justice), an attitude of discipline the likes of which I've never experienced before. Furthermore, the minimum daily adult requirement, as touching upon page count, will be eight per day.

Upon completion of the project, I will print myself a certificate, throw a party, and tell as many people as I can what I have accomplished- most of whom will either not believe me, or give me a funny look before glancing at their watches and telling me they have to go- somewhere, anywhere but here- since my crazed look is making them uncomfortable.

The writing manual I was perusing last night mentioned this type of project, and at the time- lying comfortably in bed and getting sleepy- I dismissed it as the ravings of some lunatic who has elevated the writing craft to that of a religion.

It isn't a question of "Will I?" or "Can I?" but more a "How can I not?" do this. Besides an aversion to revision, the main thing I've been missing out on is the daily habit of writing a significant amount of stuff, whether it be crap or gold. Thirty days of word-scribbling should definitely develop the writing habit.

As to content I haven't a clue. Maybe I'll go off on a hundred different tangents. Maybe the result will be one huge story. But, by any means, I'll have written a book-length work, whether it's five parts dreck, or four-parts unintelligible babbling, and one-part gold. All I know is that I can't get there unless I begin here.

So, where do I start? Surely not at the beginning, because I don't have a beginning to start from- only this spot in the notebook, which, technically, is a beginning. So, what am I talking about? What I'm afraid will happen is that this will be another one of those impulsive projects I take on, where there's a lot of hustle and bustle at the beginning, followed by what I believe to be a well-deserved breather, and after a fatal loss of momentum, the project will come to a permanent halt. And the longer the project sits there, the more mass it gains, making it harder, with each passing day, to overcome inertia. The sad thing is that the more times I don't finish a project, the lower the expectation bar is, the next time around. It gets to the point where it's more fun to start a project, especially when you know that somewhere, deep in the back of your mind, you never intended to finish the darned thing.

But maybe this time will be different. After all, I have stayed with the jury duty thing, committed to seeing it through- though it will cost me dearly. Then again, there's a difference between doing something you can't get out of, and beginning something you not only can get out of, but probably will, if your lazier self has anything to say about it. That's why structure and a system and a deadline are so important. There's got to be some sort of payoff at the end of the line- something that gives meaning and form to your project or quest. For me, the payoff is a promise that what I have embarked upon will make a better man and writer out of me. As to content, I'll just have to throw stuff at the page and see what sticks.

After lunch, the trial resumes. Galahad questions a member of an investment banking firm, and a venture capital funds manager. I struggle to understand what they're talking about, but when they speak of conflicts of interest, and failure to meet a standard of care, I perk up. They're referring to Mr. X and the slipshod (or intentional) manner in which he handled investor funds. Possible damages due to lost investment opportunities are estimated to be $16,900,000. This day in court ends in a haze of financial jargon. I am again at sea as to the specifics of the case, and it pisses me off.

11:15 p.m. Am I behind on the new writing project? Well, it sorta looks like it. I would have been well on my way to being finished if it hadn't been for the two hours of TV I watched this evening. First it was Perry Mason, then The Invaders. So, on the first day I've already screwed up- but hey, I'm back again.

"Now what?" he says, whistling. A comedy? A mystery? Tragedy? History? Drama? Sci-fi? CRAP. I should have read the manual's fine print a little more carefully. It looks like the idea is to write a novel in thirty days- not just a bunch of mish-mashed crap. I refuse to give up on this 250-pager, though. There's got to be something I can sink my teeth into. I can't keep lying here on my bed. I've got to come up with something, dammit. But, do I carry on with that something I started a while back, or try something new?

I'm getting stressed out now. Guess when you get right down to it, I don't have the guts to jump in.

Fine! Then I'm going back to 1975...

The Dodge Polara's loaded up, and I'm leaving town soon. It's just after Christmas and I've made up my mind: no more pot smoking, no more drinking and coughing up blood, no more crappy friends who either don't respect me, or instead humor me, or don't understand my desire to return to the spiritual life. They watched me go down the tubes. They were there at the start, when I stumbled and fell. They talked me into going to that X-rated movie. And I remember joking about it afterwards ...

Two pages later I quit.

Day 14

Friday, May 30

CIRCUIT COURT OF THE STATE OF XXXXXXX

To Whom It May Concern:

Since Wednesday, May 7, Daniel Hiland has been serving as a juror in a civil trial at the County Courthouse. His presence is required at the Courthouse from 8:00 a.m. until 5 p.m. daily. Current estimates by the Court indicate that the trial will last through Friday June 13. Jurors may be required to serve longer depending on the needs of the Court.

Please excuse Mr. Hiland's absence from work throughout the duration of the trial.

Please contact our court if you have any questions regarding jury service.

Sincerely,

Jane Doe

Judicial Clerk for Judge XXXXXXXX

GALAHAD QUESTIONS AN EXPERT WITNESS- a woman who specializes in loan valuation- and for once we're getting some substantive answers about how screwed up Mr. X was. After examining thousands of documents related to Mr. X's business transactions, she opines that X's business plans for one of the involved companies are some of the weakest she's ever seen. Based on the time they were drawn up, they lacked credibility or logic, were based on unsuccessful technology, utilized a weak marketing plan, and were dependent on a company that hadn't made a profit in over ten years. The witness ends by pointing out that some of CBs investments were so bad that the investors deserved their money back, with interest.

Day 15

Monday, June 2

FOLLOWING THE COURT'S INSTRUCTIONS to not appear for duty until 1:30 pm, I go to work for a couple hours. I also arrange (by phone) to have $5000 removed from my 401K to cover lost wages. Then I drive to the credit union to cash my check from the court. Rushing home, I catch the bus downtown, eat lunch at the City Café, and make my way to the jury room. After a while, another juror shows up and we chat for a few minutes. Soon, Marie the bailiff enters, surprised to see us.

"Oh, hello. The judge wanted me to inform you that you're not needed today."

"What?" I reply. "We were told to appear at 1:30."

"I left messages with everybody." She must have called after I left for the bus. Cursing under my breath, then out loud once Marie is gone, I stomp down the stairs, head to the bus stop and board a few minutes later. I pay the fare, then notice the transfer ticket in my hand.

As for the thirty-day writing project, tragedy strikes, as recorded in my journal:

> *At this point I have decided to start over. Yes, yes, I can hear you all now, saying "I knew it. I knew it wouldn't last-you'd crap out." But I have a defense. I didn't think I chose the right genre for a writing project of this scope. Because I was*

doing a memoir, I had to keep trying to remember when or where or how things happened …

I draw a large X through the above entry.

Day 16

Tuesday, June 3

RAINING HARD THIS MORNING. Make the climb up the white, pitted, worn courthouse stairs, clutching a microwaved ham-and-egg breakfast sandwich in one hand, a Pepsi and a box of Red Whip licorice in my coat pocket, umbrella and satchel in the other hand. Word is that the trial will be over a week from this coming Friday.

The defense attorneys are up first, and boring as hell. After the first hour I'm nodding off something fierce. Even after a blessed break, the blather is hard to stay focused on; I'm being persuaded to believe something that goes against my instincts- considering that a major witness is lying his ass off.

I'd rather be home, binge-watching The Invaders. I've come to a disturbing episode that sums up the series and its hero's plight. David Vincent is in a jam. He's stumbled upon a landing site in the desert, and has snuck aboard the spacecraft- even disabled it. But now he needs law enforcement and other witnesses there to capture the vehicle. He sends poor Dabney Coleman for help. I say "poor," because this is DC's second appearance in the series, and usually the second time around means death for that actor's character. Dabney goes to town and rounds up a couple cops and another man, and they head back. Somehow the aliens discover the plot, and make sure that one of the cops is an alien. Just before the car reaches the site, the alien policeman slaps a killer disk on another passenger's neck, killing him. A fight ensues and the car plunges off an embankment, crashing. But two of the passengers are still alive. One of them tries reaching for door release, but falls back, exhausted. Then the aliens show up and disintegrate the car and its occupants with a death ray.

Day 17

Wednesday, June 4

TROUBLE SLEEPING THROUGH THE NIGHT. I wake up thinking it's 5 am, but when I crane my neck for a look, the glowing red numbers say "1:30." Even in that sleepy state I have the presence of mind to curse, then struggle and finally fall asleep. But it's a restless slumber, and in the back of my mind is the fear that this is the day I'll nod off in the middle of someone's testimony or cross-examination. Maybe the sleep deficit is due to my dreams, which have been vivid and lively every night this week. I attribute this to the intellectual stimulation I'm engaged in while sitting in the jury box.

When I wake up and get ready to head for the bus stop, splintered portions of dream memory hover close by for me to grab ahold of, should I wish to. But I don't have time. Once on the bus, I relax and the nocturnal scenes slip away, even though I feel their residue. It's as if I'd been active all night, but now can't remember a damned thing.

The trial starts off with Mr. X, King of the Prevaricators, on the stand. I wonder how I'm going to stay awake-then I drift off like Alice under that tree. Moments later I awake in a stupor and begin scribbling the first words that come into my head- and it's about the psychological makeup of Mr. X:

> ... *"he was so lonely that any positive attention paid to him was soaked up like a sponge. Having spent so many years without what most would consider "normal, healthy friendships," every potential long-term human interaction was viewed as binary. Black or white. Either this woman is going to become a girlfriend- or I'll be civil and friendly, but move away from her as soon as possible. So, later in life, those who would approach him in a friendly manner were in for disappointment. The number of things attached- mostly invisible, under his surface- got in the way of what could have been a great friendship. Being lonely for so long, things had gotten to the point where his "buckets" would never be filled, no matter how much attention he was paid. He didn't know how to deal with that kind of attention"* ...

But when I read closely, the description could just as easily be of me. No matter, though. At least I'm awake again- though for how long I'm uncertain, as a new threat to consciousness appears. Mr. X is speaking in a gentle, almost monotone, voice, while demonstrating his inability to use simple language. What I hear is a soothing tone at an easy cadence, with long and complex phraseology that has a progressively numbing effect on the brain:

leverage
strategy
technology

hosting
corporations
streamlined
consolidate
bubble burst
analytical
given
determining
internet
information managing
behavior
consumer
comprehensive
processing
acquired
core product
offering
variety
modest
recovery
majority
focused
environment
systems
firm
enable
format
digital
issue
two-fold
contract
overhaul
downturn

content
provider
measured
correct
sufficient

As grey cells are beaten into submission, Eels meanwhile subjects Mr. X to a series of questions designed to elicit sympathy from the troops.

"I did my best for the investors."

"Yes, I borrowed millions from the investors, and concealed it. But I always intended to repay the debts-and I did so."

"There are still some winners in the portfolio."

Then Mr. X gets teary-eyed and contrite.

"I'm sorry. I know that my actions have caused great pain to my family and my reputation."

Well, I don't buy it. Last week Galahad asked Mr. X why he couldn't bring himself to admit that he'd stolen the funds. Mr. X looked him straight in the eye and said the transactions were loans to him, not theft. The man is in denial. Does his attorney think we're stupid? While referring to a key witness, Mr. X says that she was a highly ethical, principled employee. I believe he hired her to take care of his books because she could do the job, not because of her stated virtues. In word and deed, Mr. X seems to regard ethics as a convenience when it suits his needs. His strength lies in persuading the wealthy and the influential to part with their money.

X's attorney goes on and on with the questions and the posturing, but nothing is more boring or aggravating than listening to someone play Cover-Your-Ass by shifting the blame. Well, as long as I keep writing I can stay awake. Gotta hold out until Galahad and Canada get a whack at him. But first we're exposed to another dose of Mr. X's linguistic cure for insomnia:

value-added
perspective
phenomenon
positive
contacts
potential
former
products
discussions
interest
channels
key
condition
achieved
process
sustainable
scale
volume
challenge

After this we're allowed a break. I walk out of the courtroom, trying to shake the verbiage out of my head. But all too soon, it's back to work.

Number Seven, to my left, has traded in his terminal bad breath for gum chewing. He gnaws on the Wrigley's, his mouth open just far enough to emit a light snapping, crackly sound that's really pissing me off. Why can't he shut his damned trap? It's a light sound, similar to the court reporter's long, white, manicured fingernails tap dancing across the laptop keyboard. But now comes another three minutes of Mr. X's verbal Novocain:

retrospect
uncertainty
viability
transfer
determined
marketplace
meaningful
analysis
diligence
acquired
timeframe
sources
verified
acquisition
write-down

Sleep is returning. I can't focus very long. But like the rescuing cavalry, one of the plaintiff's attorneys now addresses the court. He reminds us why we're here: most of the $75,000,000 that Mr. X got his grubby mitts on is gone; investors are suing for breach of fiduciary duty as a result of Mr. X borrowing millions from investor funds to pay off his incurred debts; investors are suing the defunct Accountants "R" Us for not alerting them when said company discovered Mr. X's actions.

During cross-examination, Canada queries Mr. X.

“When you borrow money, wouldn’t you agree that the lender should know that it is making the loan? If the lender doesn’t know, how is it different from embezzlement?”

“I always intended to pay it back, and I have.”

“How about the $175,000 of investor funds that you steered into one account, then removed $100,000 of to pay a photographer who was following that year’s presidential candidates?

“It was a stupid thing. I don’t know why it got done.”

“I have no further questions of this witness, your Honor.”

Skipped my second-to-the last writing class this evening. Sore throat. Slight fever. Spaciness. The usual crap. Slept from 7 - 10 pm, then from 1 - 6 am.

Day 18

Thursday, June 5

ENDLESS JURY DUTY CONTINUES. Sitting here at the bus stop- the better one, since it has two seats and some shelter- I'm grateful that it's not raining. Bus stops aren't the best places to write, though, as I'm always on guard. If I concentrate too much on scribbling, I'll be unprepared when the bus comes. So, it's write, look, write, look...

Told Number Eleven, a few days ago, that serving jury duty makes me feel smarter. Probably because I have to focus my attention on testimony concerning financial transactions and complicated concepts all day long. And all the while I find that in order to make sense of it all, I have to compare what I'm hearing with what's already been said. Then I try to determine if it's true or just crap. And there's plenty of the latter to wade through. I've taken tons of notes. Somewhere along the line I'll need to put them into a timeline to make sense of them. My wife continues to sock away the trial articles from the daily paper. Guess I'll find out after it's all over just how close we jurors were to the mark, or if we made some horrible mistake during deliberations.

I've only been on the stand a few minutes when my lower regions start to rumble. I'm hoping this isn't what I think it is. Well, the first pain has come and gone.

Maybe that was it. Then Wave #2 comes and goes, no big deal. Afterward, all is calm and peaceful. A new witness- whoever he is- has been sworn in and is answering questions. But I'm having trouble concentrating.

Oh, oh. Here come Waves #3 and #4. A couple minutes later Wave #5 stops by for a visit, the pain getting worse. What the hell did I eat for breakfast? Is this punishment for some terrible sin I committed?

Wave #6 pulls into the station, right on schedule. It's starting to feel like an impending diarrhea attack, and I'm stuck here in the jury box- all gassed up, with nowhere to go. I look at the stand and see the witness and attorney conversing, but I can't concentrate on a damned thing they're saying.

Lucky #7 comes- and eventually goes. But it really hurts. As it subsides, I try to maintain outward calm, while deep inside, my gut gurgles and rumbles. Goose bumps and a clammy film of cold sweat form on my skin. All is quiet on the southern front for a minute or two. Another ten minutes pass. Could it be that I've paid the price? Maybe I've been spared.

Then #8 hits, the demonic internal pressure building to a crescendo like some sinister gastrointestinal symphony- before mercifully subsiding. I look at the clock and wish its hands would move faster. Before I can get my breath, though, #9 comes knocking with Braxton-Hicks regularity. As the internal pressure builds and backs up, builds and backs up, the goose bumps return and my face feels flush and I wonder how much longer I can hold off a horribly messy, albeit historical, accident in the jury box. The only bright spot now is that the pain is keeping me awake.

Then a miracle occurs. The judge has called for morning recess. Faster than you can say "ulcerative colitis," I make a beeline for the Blessed Stall down on the fourth floor. After an explosive session on the commode, I'm a new man.

More observations surface from jurors about the nose-picking habits of a few of the attorneys. One fellow in particular was seen using the end of his pen like a swizzle stick, cleaning out one of his nostrils. The Scrabble games and tie updates continue, as well as derogatory comments about how strange some of the witnesses look. Then again, when one is stuck in a jury seat for six hours a day, the mind is bound to wander. Little sounds like the pop of a bumped microphone, or coughing, or the sound of bagpipes (coming from the street below), break the tension, but also one's concentration. And while I'm a little hard of hearing, my nose works all too well. I'm getting more and more sensitized to the stereo bad breath coming from Jurors Five and Seven. The former's is a tooth decay update every time she yawns, the latter's kimchee bouquet more furtive, sneaking through the air like an olfactory guerilla. I've learned something useful today, though. When I start feeling sleepy, all I need to do is start writing in Spanish. The fringe benefit of this is that no one can read what I've written. Including me.

Get to leave an hour early today. A good thing, as sleep deficit is having its way with me.

Day 19

Friday, June 6

IT'S BEEN OVER A MONTH since I first reported for jury duty. Guess I got my wish, with a vengeance. Had a crappy night's sleep, much of which was spent tossing and turning and blowing my nose, non-stop. Don't know how I'm going to stay awake for the trial.

Turns out that it isn't that bad. Plaintiff's attorney is doing the questioning. After a while, we're sent off on an extended lunch hour. I stop by a run-down bookstore, then wander the aisles of Borders for a while.

By afternoon the opposing parties have rested, meaning that we're done listening to testimony. And not a moment too soon. Closing arguments should begin on Monday. Then the real fun begins.

The judge lets us go at 4 pm, but I remain in the jury room, assembling a time line in a spare steno pad. I'm trying to make sense out of all the events that occurred over a thirteen-year period. After an hour of that I catch a bus for home.

Closing Arguments

Day 20

Monday June 9

LEFT EARLY FOR WHAT MAY BE THE LAST DAY of jury duty. But I wonder. There's so much evidence to plow through that it'll take hours just to assemble it into some meaningful order. The first challenge of the day will be staying awake.

I don't know why, but Carol and I have been having trouble sleeping, the last three nights. Being sick with a cold doesn't help. I have some sort of bronchial condition, but with a twist. A wheeze has developed, one that comes with a repertoire of sounds- like bronchial bagpipes. A variety of tones happen on the inhale, a different set for the exhale. Sometimes, I'll be lying in bed and think I'm hearing the sounds of an animal in distress- like a rabbit crying its last, at the mercy of our stupid cat or a raccoon- only to discover it's my bronchial tubes whining forlornly. Occurring at the distant ends of the respiratory spectrum, the whistling follows a moment of calm and easy breathing, making it hard to fall asleep because I know it's coming. It's worse when I lay on my left side, not so bad on the right. Being this congested, the lungs rattling with each deep breath, I have a hard time telling when I've inhaled far enough, thus making it harder than hell to relax. But eventually the body finds a way. I fall off for at least a few hours of shuteye before waking too early, then enduring a long session of toss-and-turn before turning on talk radio and zoning out.

I take a seat on the bus next to a middle-aged woman. She offers a "Good morning," something people don't usually say in this place or time. The norm for me is to keep myself from jostling or bumping into the other person, no matter how much the bus sways and lurches. But this lady is more civil than most. Wearing a thin, dark coat, her jet-black hair is all large curls stuffed up under a stocking cap that more than contains it all. I open my notebook and start writing. I've done a half-page when I notice she's watching me.

"You must be a good writer, to keep on the page the way this bus is moving around."

"Yeah," I say, grateful for the attention. I love to talk to people about my writing.

"I try to write every day so I can keep in practice. Otherwise I'll stop."

"Um-hmm," she says, staring ahead instead of out the window, a sign she wants to talk some more.

"Do you write?"

"Well, I used to, but my hand, it won't work very..." Her words trail off to a mumble as she lifts her right hand, palm up. At first glance it looks just like the other. Until she tries to move her fingers. The digits twitch slightly, but that's it.

"I can hardly move my fingers any more. The doctor said that in a few years they'll be better. Yes, I used to write some letters and stuff."

She sounds tired but her eyes glitter.

"What happened?" I ask. "You have an accident?"

"Well," she says, slow and deliberate, the fingers of her left hand caressing the right wrist, "I was working near some glass one day, and I slipped and got cut bad."

She holds the wounded hand up higher. The wrist looks blocky, squared off, bones enlarged and uneven, the surrounding skin a mass of lumps.

"So, you cut some tendons or…"

"Cut her clean off."

"Your whole hand?" I was aghast.

"Yep. It was just hangin' by a little piece of skin here." She's pointing to her wrist again. "It happened 'bout two years ago. My fingers tingle a little bit, but I can't use this hand yet."

Aside from a few oh-mans, a "Do you work?" is the best I can come up with.

"No. Can't do much without this hand."

"So, how do you get by? Disability?"

"When I'se in the hospital they tried to get me on disability, but I didn't want it, no."

She reaches up with her good hand and pulls the cable. "Good talking to you" she says, and is off the bus before I can reply.

I exit the bus at 7:10 and several blocks too soon. Still not used to the street layout, even after a month of doing this, I think it's got a lot to do with the distracting nature of the cityscape. Stores and businesses and people of every color, shape and size. As I head up the sidewalk, destination City Café, I inhale deeply, lungs rattling with every draw. Forcing out a long, phlegm-clearing hack, I spit, sensing a strong metallic aftertaste. This cold isn't done with me yet. Breakfast is good. Bacon and cheese omelet, hash browns, toast and juice.

THE MORNING STARTS WITH CANADA, all spiffed up, hair slicked back, wearing a three-piece suit. He approaches the podium. Full of emotion, he speaks to us of the critical part we jurors play in this trial. For the next ninety minutes, he reminds us who caused the damage to his clients, as well as when, how and why: that the Canadian investors lost most of the $51,000,000 they invested with Mr. X. Canada produces a display board bearing the title "The Shell Game." Upon this he places three faux plastic turtle shells. He slides each shell around the board to show how money was moved from one fund to another, much of it ending up in Mr. X's pocket. He displays a box full of puzzle pieces, illustrating how hard it is to solve, when you only have three or four pieces out the original two-thousand. He finishes by quoting from the book "Bird by Bird," where the author says that when one is faced with a huge task, tackle one thing at a time.

Galahad's next. Less emotional but more analytical, he talks a lot about how Accountants "R" Us had a hand in the deceptions that took place. The most interesting part of his presentation is a discussion about the Statute of Limitations and its relationship to the damages incurred by the investors. Then we recess an hour for lunch.

At 1:30, Mr. Eels (X's attorney) presents his argument. I find him fairly boring, and see a lot more merit in the plaintiff's side of the case. Not mentioning the fact that his client misused millions of dollars of investor cash, Eels tries to persuade us that the plaintiffs are merely money hungry, and accuses the investors of "waging the best case that money can buy." He goes on about the Statute of Limitations. He ends his argument by telling us that we have the power to find Mr. X guilty, but we will be violating our oath as jurors if we do not first consider all the facts. Duh. I'm reminded of why lawyers make such good politicians: their ability to stretch and bend and otherwise manipulate the truth to suit their needs.

Rueful, the Accountants "R" Us attorney, then addresses us. He reminds us that jurors are important because they bring the real world into the courtroom. His arguments are by far the most boring of the bunch. As it's 3:20, I hope he hurries things up so the plaintiff's rebuttal can finish in time. But Rueful goes on and on, repeating the assertion that plaintiffs are going after his client because of the deep pockets Accountants "R" Us had. The longer he talks, the less I listen. As his argument winds down, he's beginning to sound whiny: "The investors refuse to take responsibility for their actions."

Following the plaintiff's rebuttal, we're released around 5 pm. It's hard to believe that this part of the trial is finally over.

I remain in the jury room after everyone leaves, so I can continue compiling the timeline of events. I hope I can get into the jury room early enough tomorrow morning to finish it. It's the only way I can make sense of this most tangled web. After thirty minutes a clerk pops her head in the door and says I need to leave, but she thinks it's smart of me to be creating that timeline.

After moving a bunch of books from the garage library into the kitchen, I make room out there for a table, chair and lamp. Then I move all of my composition books and other writing stuff out there. I really do need a dedicated place where I can sit and develop better writing habits. Gotta find a way to force or coerce myself into working on revisions.

Another six-hour night of sleep lies ahead …

Deliberations

Day 21

Tuesday, June 10

GRAY AND OVERCAST THIS MORNING, in the middle fifties, you'd think it was fall. Back at the City Café for maybe the last time. It'll be an omelet, hash browns, toast and fruit juice, like yesterday. It's 7:15, and amidst the surrounding buildings and the tree-lined park, it's dark and dusk-like. Soon I'm in the JR, working on the time line.

At 9 am we file into the courtroom and the judge begins reading the Verdict Form. Word for word. It's an eleven-page set of jury instructions, complete with the forms we need to fill out. It begins with definitions and the rules of the game, so to speak:

> *"At least the same nine jurors must agree to the answers for each of the questions relating to Mr. X."*
>
> *"At least the same nine jurors must agree to the answers for each of the questions relating to Accountants "R" Us"*

"Unless otherwise stated, "plaintiffs" refers to the parties related to Funds I, II, III" (and the two Canadian funds).

"Unless otherwise stated, "defendants" refers to Mr. X Company, Inc (I, II, and III), and Mr. X and Associates, Inc."

After we deliberate about all the salient points, we are to enter our findings, as a jury- said findings broken down into five sections, and represented by "Yes" or "No" questions and damage amounts:

I. Claims Against Mr. X

1. Did Mr. X convert plaintiffs' money, and, if so, was it a cause of damage to plaintiffs?
2. Did Mr. X breach a fiduciary duty owed to plaintiffs, and, if so, was it a cause of damage to plaintiffs?
3. Was Mr. X negligent?
4. Did Mr. X make a negligent misrepresentation?
5. Did Mr. X breach a contract with plaintiffs?
6. Did Mr. X breach an implied covenant of good faith and fair dealings with plaintiffs?
7. Did Mr. X breach a contract to provide the Canadian plaintiffs with audited financial statements?

At this point, the questionnaire stops to introduce confusion into the mix:

"If you answered "No" to all of the above questions 1 – 7, your verdict is for Mr. X. Proceed to question 11 in Section II."

"If you answered "Yes" to any of the above questions, proceed to question 8. At least the same nine jurors who answered "Yes" to any of the above questions must also agree on the answers to any of questions 8 – 10 in which you award damages."

8. What are plaintiffs' money damages, if any, caused by Mr. X's conversion, breach of fiduciary duty, negligence, and/or negligent misrepresentation?

ANSWER for Fund I:

Money taken by Mr. X: $_________
Mr. X. and Associates Management Fees: $_________
Accountants "R" Us Fees: $_________
Payments to Canadian funds: $_________

ANSWER for Fund II:

Money taken by Mr. X: $_________
Mr. X. and Associates Management Fees: $_________
Accountants "R" Us Fees: $_________
Payments to Canadian funds: $_________

ANSWER for Fund III:

Money taken by Mr. X: $_________
Mr. X. and Associates Management Fees: $_________
Accountants "R" Us Fees: $_________
Payments to Canadian funds: $_________

(The total money damage awarded in question 8 may not exceed $45,000.28.)

And the judge reads on …

9. What are the plaintiffs' money damages, if any, caused by Mr. X's breach of contract and/or breach

of the implied covenant of good faith and fair dealing?

ANSWER for Fund I:

Money taken by Mr. X: $________
Mr. X. and Associates Management Fees: $________
Accountants “R” Us Fees: $________

ANSWER for Fund II:

Money taken by Mr. X: $________
Mr. X. and Associates Management Fees: $________
Accountants “R” Us Fees: $________

ANSWER for Fund III:

Money taken by Mr. X: $________
Mr. X. and Associates Management Fees: $________
Accountants “R” Us Fees: $________

10. What are the money damages Mr. X caused the Canadian funds?

ANSWER:
$________

(Total money damage awarded in Question 10 may not exceed $23,537.)

II. Claims Against Accountants "R" Us

11. Did Accountants "R" Us breach a contract with plaintiffs?
12. Was Accountants "R" Us negligent?
13. Did Accountants "R" Us commit fraud?
14. Is Accountants "R" Us liable to plaintiffs for negligent misrepresentation?
15. What are plaintiffs' money damages, if any, caused by Accountants "R" Us?

By this time, I've mentally checked out. But the judge reads on and on …

III. Restatement Section 876

16. Is Accountants "R" Us liable for the wrongful conduct of Mr. X, under Restatement Section 876(a)?
17. Is Accountants "R" Us liable for the wrongful conduct of Mr. X, under Restatement Section 876(b)?
18. Is Accountants "R" Us liable for the wrongful conduct of Mr. X, under Restatement Section 876(c)?

"If you answered "No" to all of the above questions 16 - 18, your verdict is for Accountants "R" Us with regard to liability for the wrongful conduct of Mr. X. Proceed to question 20 in Section IV."

"If you answered "Yes" to any of the above questions 16 - 18, proceed to question 19. At least the same nine jurors who answered "Yes" to any of

the above questions must also agree on the answers to question 19.

19. What are the plaintiffs' money damages, if any, caused my Mr. X's wrongful conduct for which Accountants "R" Us is liable under Restatement Section 876(c)?

IV. Punitive Damages

20. Should punitive damages be awarded against Mr. X?

21. Should punitive damages be awarded against Accountants "R" Us?

V. Defenses

22. Were plaintiffs negligent in one or more of the ways claimed by Mr. X or Accountant's "R" Us, and if so, was plaintiff's negligence a cause of damages to themselves?

23. Are the plaintiffs' claim for breach of contract and breach of the implied covenant of good faith and fair dealing against Mr. X, and plaintiffs' claims for conversion against Mr. X barred by the six-year statute of limitation?

24. Are the plaintiffs' claims against Mr. X for breach of fiduciary duty, negligence, and negligent misrepresentation barred by the two-year statute of limitation?

25. Are the plaintiffs' claims for breach of contract, professional negligence, negligent misrepresentation, fraud, and Section 876 liability against Defendant Accountant's "R" Us barred by the two-year statute of limitation?

26. Were plaintiffs *in pari delicto* with Accountants "R" Us?

The presiding juror should sign and date this form.

I've never seen anything like this. It takes the judge half an hour to go through, the effort an exercise in futility. We the jury will need to pore over this document many times to makes sense of it.

His current duty done, the judge swears in the two bailiffs and excuses us from the courtroom. Armed with scores of documents and a million questions, we toddle off to the JR, the two alternates dismissed. I feel sorry for them. They've been attentive- more so than a couple of the regular jurors- taking copious notes and remaining aware of what's been said all through the trial. I wonder how disappointed or relieved they are.

We order lunch, knowing we're in for a long haul. Then it's time to elect a foreman. Number Four suggests that I assume that position. I'm flattered, as this is a sign that some of the other jurors respect me and my perceived ability. But a combination of low self-esteem and a lack of confidence in what this trial is all about cause me to decline. We end up voting for Number Ten, the man with management experience. While I feel a sense of relief at not being in charge, the wisdom of my choice to decline is one I will come to question by trial's end.

As we begin, self-appointed roles are assumed. Number Ten has been chosen for his leadership skills, and his straightforward approach to the facts. Number One, good reading skills, which help her find the facts quickly.

Number Eleven, a desire for order, moving her to form lists and a voting record. Number Four, while not speaking much, steps forward occasionally with a well-thought-out reason for voting as he does, backed by solid evidence. Due to my talent for organizing disparate bits of data into information, I've assembled the timeline. And what would any jury be without a couple of naysayers? People who seem to say "No" every time another says "Yes." Number Eight, an immigrant with a troubled past, is so biased, so bitter, that she refuses to participate in our decision-making. She despises the United States legal system, and takes every opportunity to denigrate it. How she ever made it past the peremptory challenges is a mystery to me. Juror Number Two runs on emotion, his stated reasons for voting as he does not making much sense. Somewhere along the line he decided that the defendants are getting a raw deal, which also makes no sense, in view of the evidence. And in the end, his emotion-based arguments are disregarded.

We start with Question #1 on the verdict form, Number One taking on the task of reading each legal definition out loud. After some discussion, we take a vote.

Day 22

Wednesday, June 11

HEADING FOR JD THIS MORNING, I'm not enthused about the prospect of spending eight hours with the rest of the gang. Before, our role was passive: sit and wait until called, then take notes and try to stay awake for the substantive bits. Then there was the noon recess and the hunt for the best eating spot. Now we have to do all the work- deciding the facts of the case. Taking notes was easy. Making sense out of them, though, is proving to be a Herculean task. There are so many, some with dates, others with Exhibit numbers, many with both, but a whole hell of a lot of them without anything more than "Letter from Mr. X to Mr. Y." Some of the more cryptic notations have been put out of their misery, a line drawn through them. Others remain there on page after page, challenging me to remember who, what, or when they are related to the rest of this stew of words. To the walls and windows I've taped the last of the twenty-four sheets of 3' by 4' poster paper that make up the timeline I've been assembling.

At lunchtime, I decide to get out of my shell and go with Numbers Four, Eleven and someone else to the Farmer's Market, a few blocks uptown from the courthouse. As we walk along, I feel some regret for not having spent more time with my fellow jurists. My habit had been to keep to myself during down times, reserving conversation for the JR itself; easier to stay up there than make the effort to get to know the others better. It's a lifelong pattern that's no doubt deprived me of many a potential friendship. That being said, I have made a few friends, this group being the most gregarious of any jurors I've been associated with. Someone made a comment earlier today about a topic we'd discussed weeks ago, and it makes me realize how long we've been together. There's been a lot of sharing. I tell a couple jurors that I consider this last five weeks to be a life-changing event. For some it's only been something to endure, but I look on this as an unforgettable experience. If for no other reason, it's been a blessing to be absent from The Company for over a month.

By afternoon, 75% of the Yes-No questions have been resolved. We recess for the rest of the day, and I'm grateful. Information overload has arrived and there's nothing left with which to reason. I'm enjoying a mindless bus ride home- until we arrive at the transit station across the river. As the bus pulls to a stop, I notice two guys sitting on a bench. One of them is finishing off a joint. A transit security officer walks their way, so one of the duo drops the smoke and snuffs it out with a weathered sneaker. I'm staring at him while watching the woman to see if she's noticed the concealment. Now the guys are both looking at me, laughing in a mocking way. I return their chuckles with a sneer and look at the security woman again. Moments later one of the potheads is at my window, cursing, his face a mask of fury and hatred as he punches the window hard, still yelling. His left hand shoots through the partially opened window, fingers clutching at the air as he tries to grab my shoulder. I'm backing up, yelling "Get outta here! Go on- get away!" while nearby passengers watch, none coming forward to assist. I slide the window closed as my new friend yanks his fingers back, the bus pulling away as he continues to shout curses. The other passengers are looking at me funny, as if I've been having a quarrel with a chum. One guy keeps staring at me.

"They were mad at me because I saw them smoking pot."

He shrugs and looks out the window, conversation over before it's even begun. He's no doubt thinking I'm a jackass for engaging with the dopehead. Or he's not thinking at all. Good thing I didn't have to depend on any of these people for my safety.

After returning home, I grab my revised story for writing class and search for the parking permit. Then I remember that I loaned it to my daughter for her night class. Irritated, I head for school, hoping the Jeep won't get towed away. My mind on other things, I miss the exit and have to take the next one, backtracking to return to the correct road. I cross the freeway, take a right and drive along a street I used to travel in the old days to get to school. Well, things have changed a lot since the old days. I come to an intersection and take a right, only to discover one mile later that it's now a dead end. Backtracking, I return to the main drag. Taking the left fork this time, I tool along until I come to another intersection and take another left. I know I'm close, but one mile after another flies by. Soon I realize I've taken yet another wrong freaking turn.

Four or five miles and batch of expletives later I come to an intersection and hang a right. Finally on the proper road, I travel a few more miles, the campus dead ahead. As usual there are no non-permit parking spaces open. Reaching the bottom of the hill, I spot a parking permit vending machine and buy a window sticker. I run across campus, into the right building, down the hallway, and into an empty classroom. There's a note on the board telling me and some guy name Jack to slide our papers under the teacher's office door. I hoof it over to his office and as luck would have it, the door is open. Walking back to his cubicle, I find him still there. After I hand over the assignment- my revised draft of a Shakespeare satire- we talk for a few minutes. I ask him what I can do to improve my writing skills.

"Well, there's really nothing I can suggest, except to focus your time on revising."

"In other words, I need to write my ass off."

"That's right."

Satisfied with his assessment, I head out, stopping buy a bar to talk with some classmates for an hour, before heading home.

Day 23

Thursday, June 12

MAKE IT TO THE BUS STOP JUST IN TIME. I'm feeling good, excited about the day ahead. There are several eight-to-ten-year old boys standing there.

"Where're you guys headed? Into the city?"

"Nah," the oldest one says.

"Well," I say, as if grade-school kids would be interested in how a middle-aged man is going to spend his day, "I'm going to jury duty downtown."

They look at each other with a "whatever" eye roll. I've said too much, but try to find a graceful way out.

"Man, this jury duty is costing me a lot of money."

They're definitely looking anywhere but at me, so as to encourage an end to the conversation. The bus arrives and I resolve to keep my mouth shut more often, around strangers.

I board #44, the same bus line I was riding yesterday when I encountered Angry Pothead. Since the odds of running into him again are next to nil, I decided to chance it.

Stop at the kiosk and get a breakfast sandwich: ham, cheese and egg, all between two muffins. She even heats it up for me.

After arriving at the jury room, I tape the timeline sheets back onto the windows and walls, so I'll have a place to sit. The table is covered with steno pads, pens lodged in the coiled wire bindings, three tall gold-and-black water pitchers (always full when we arrive in the morning), water bottles, pop cans and paper coffee cops everywhere, assorted pens here and there, boxes of chips and crackers, and bags of chocolate. What's been added to the mess now are evidence books, copies of the verdict forms, and that eleven-page set of jury instructions. The ever-present coffee-maker continues to brew the elixir that everyone bitches about but many continue to drink. Crappy coffee is better than none, I guess.

The formerly silent Juror Seven got here just after I did and he's digging though the evidence books. I don't get it. He sits there like a lump through all the deliberations, and doesn't say jack. When we vote, he abstains. Or votes "No." He contributes nary a single question, yet now he wants everything explained to him. On our last day, he's suddenly the busy bee. When he asks me about fees, I shrug my shoulders, unwilling to help him.

WE'RE INTO THE MONEY PORTION of the session now, and I'm frigging lost. I've asked a couple times about what the hell is going on, but haven't received any answers- so I push my chair back and sulk, pissed off, after which I disengage from the discussion. Maybe I shouldn't be mad, but instead thankful for a break from the proceedings. I contributed a lot earlier, so I should just chill. But having to admit that I'm a dunce about something that others seem to be easily understanding makes me feel bad.

It's getting close to lunchtime and there's been a breakthrough: everybody gets to put their suggested damage amounts on a list. Then we'll look for consensus. Juror Ten and I are the only ones who want to stay with the damage amounts the plaintiffs are asking for. Just after 3 pm we arrive at an agreement on the numbers. After an hour's work the figures are tabulated. Then they're checked and double-checked.

At 6 pm we're called into the courtroom, nervous as cats. We file past a full gallery to the left, lawyers and staff to the right, all eyes fixed on us. The judge welcomes us back to the land of the living. First order of business is the reading of the verdict. As he moves from one question to the next, I watch the poker-faced attorneys. They're filling in each line on the verdict form. So far, so good. After the last question, the judge tells us to prepare for "polling," and my anxiety level inches up a notch. I once heard of a trial where everything was moving along, smooth as you please. Then, during polling (where the judge asks each juror how they voted), one hapless juror became confused. This juror said he'd voted one way when he'd actually voted the opposite. A mistrial was declared.

Our judge begins.

"How many of the jurors voted "Yes" for Question 1?" We show by a raise of hands. Like a sightseer wondering if he should jump from the high bridge he's standing on, I wonder how much trouble I'd cause if I forget how I voted. The judge moves methodically from Question 2 to Question 3, and so on and so on. All is well until some point prior to Question 26, when Juror Seven, to my left, fails to raise his hand with the rest of us. After counting again, the judge looks at the confused fellow.

"How did you vote? Yes or No?"

Now what? Is all our work getting flushed down the drain due to this guy's brain-dead answers? Number Seven hems. Number Seven haws. Then-

"I'm not sure."

He's not *sure*? He was sure, before. What the hell is wrong with this guy?

"I uh- emm- err..."

Suddenly, the Question Lady, speaks up.

"Your Honor?"

Why is Number Three shoving her oar in?

"Yes?"

"Juror Seven has abstained."

Abstained. So now she's a legal scholar.

"Abstained, huh?" the judge says. He makes a note of it and moves on. All I can see, hear, and think is MISTRIAL, MISTRIAL, MISTRIAL.

The judge continues polling each of us. Every time he asks for a count, I watch Juror Seven with fear and trembling; with every vote he glances up and down the front row to see how everyone else is voting. Then he raises his hand.

Somehow, we make it to the end. The judge excuses us for a few minutes, then summons us back.

"Thank you for your efforts to come to a determination about the verdict."

I finally relax, assuming that the judge has seen through Juror Seven's jackassery. Then-

"Before we recess for the day, the jury will need to return tomorrow to calculate the punitive damages to be awarded against Mr. X. Thank you."

Extra innings.

Standing by the bus stop a short time later, I see a brightly colored cyclist gliding down the street, a city bus braking as it tries to maintain a healthy distance between its front bumper and her rear one. Wearing a feathered helmet, head held high, flags and feathers flapping in the wind, the woman appears parade-ready and the picture of bliss. It's the Question Lady.

Punitive Damages

Day 24

Friday, June 13

SUNNY, BEAUTIFUL SPRING DAY. Nice big article on the front page of the paper which I'm not supposed to read yet. One part of me doesn't want this JD to end; the other part realizes it's time to return to the real world. The latter part is also telling me that while there are still some challenges ahead, the service I've endured will better prepare me to deal with problems at The Company.

After we're seated in the box, the judge speaks.

"I'll remind the jury that having found the defendants guilty, you now need to agree on a fixed amount of punitive damages. In order to fairly determine this amount, more testimony needs to be elicited about the financial condition of the accused."

Canada calls Mr. X to the stand.

"Do you continue to manage funds?"

"Yes."

"What is your yearly gross revenue?"

"$500,000."

"What is your personal salary?"

"$300,000."

"How many shares of XXX stock do you own?"

"One million."

"Do you own a home?"

"Yes. 8,500-10,000 square feet."

"How much is it worth?"

"$4,000,000."

Canada speaks.

"Ladies and gentlemen of the jury. This trial has been hard on all of us, but it's been necessary. As a jury, it is your job to send a message about what is and is not "okay" behavior. The defendant has shown a blatant disregard for the people who trusted him with their money. As you make a determination of the damage amount, consider the duration of Mr. X's conduct. It took place over a ten-year period, during which he kept telling little lies. In essence, Mr. X belongs to a class of people who take other people's money in trust- but it is a system that can fall apart through a lack of integrity."

After elaborating on the extent of Mr. X's offenses, Canada thanks us and sits down, as Mr. X returns to his seat.

Mr. Eels approaches the podium. Looking crestfallen, contrite and disappointed, he speaks in a barely audible voice. The defendant is sitting at his assigned desk, eyes fixed on the attorney's every move. I continue to watch Mr. X, wondering if he's afraid to look anywhere else, when his glance drops to the table, then up and into my eyes. We stare at each other for eight long seconds, neither of us willing to break away- then his gaze shifts back to the man speaking. I've seen nothing in those eyes that resembles humility or pleading; more a cold, soulless stare, some loathing and contempt thrown in for good measure. The attorney's words come and go, but don't register. I have no sympathy for the defendant, my only desire being to finish him and the trial.

Canada returns.

"Please remember the power you hold in your hands. Your job is to send a message to every corner of the state."

And I'm more than ready to do just that. Following some brief words of instruction, the judge sends us forth to deliberate one more time. After believing we were done, this is a bit rough. You would think that once a person learns a new skill or a new way of thinking about complex things, he or she would jump at the opportunity to use those skills again- as if the mind is holding an open house, and it's been given the chance to show off a newly opened section of the brain. But such enthusiasm is not present, judging by the looks on our faces as we trudge out of the jury box, exit the courtroom for the hallway- one last official trip back to our litigatory home away from home.

We sit down on those hard wooden chairs and consider the two forms before us. While much shorter than the previous ones, these papers will document our decision about how much of a financial ass-kicking Mr. X and Accountants "R" Us deserve. According to the Jury Instructions, we are to take seven factors into consideration, including Mr. X's motive, the character of his conduct, how long his misconduct and concealment of same lasted, Mr. X's conduct upon being caught in the act, and so on and so on. Lots of food for thought, there. I take a gander at the verdict form. Only five lines to fill in, but no dollar amounts assigned. Nothing to go by. It looks like we'll be here for a while longer.

We settle in and talk about how large the punitive damages should be. Then we try to come up with a maximum penalty. But, like trying to paint a mural with no idea of what the finished picture should look like, we're stymied. Finally, I speak up, suggesting $20,000,000. No one wants to go that high.

"How about $1.00?" suggests Juror Eight, the immigrant with an anvil-sized political chip on her shoulder. She takes a dim view of the American legal process, and the jury system in particular. But no matter. Since she refused to participate in the voting before, all she can do now is run her mouth.

"Mr. X has suffered enough."

"No," I tell her. He hasn't suffered enough,"

And many agree with me. Maybe it's the inflammatory, cynical nature of Number Eight's remarks. We've been enduing her increasingly negative, sour-grapes attitude, the nearer we come to trial's end. Maybe it's because others are starting to feel guilty for not having spoken sooner. But, for whatever reason, formerly quiet jurors are now spurred to action.

"I think Dan's twenty-million figure is pretty close to the mark," says one.

"Well, I think it should be more like four million," says another. Others pipe up, leaning toward something in the middle. But at least we're talking. Analysis paralysis is no more. We have a frame of reference to work within.

Back and forth we go. After a time, someone- using the same system we developed before, where discussion points were written on a large sheet of paper- starts tallying and listing everyone's suggested dollar amounts, in descending order. My 20,000,000 reigns at the top, Number Eight's ludicrous $1.00 figure squashed flat at the bottom by the weight of common sense. Amounts recorded and on display, we take turns explaining why our respective figures best represent a just amount, based on the Seven Items to Consider. Since we've had a lot of practice with this method, we finish in a fraction of the time it took before. An amount settled on, we vote. The same ten of us agree, as before, with Juror Eight having thankfully thrown in the ideological towel. The foreman then fills out and signs the verdict form.

There's a small button on the wall that needs to be pressed to call the bailiff. We give that honor to the youthful Juror Five, the Girl Who Slept In, so long ago. She's delighted, and gives the button a push. Then we're filing out of the JR for our last official journey to the courtroom. As we come into court and sit, a feeling of relief washes over me. The obligation to do anything more than relax is gone. The judge reads the verdict while plaintiff's lawyers and a reporter or two scribble like mad- unlike counsel for the defense, who are quickly realizing there's nothing but bad news for their side. The judge thanks us for our service and excuses us from what has been the longest civil trial the judge and some of the attorneys have ever experienced.

The sum total of our labors?

1) Mr. X is proven guilty of taking money from three failed venture capital funds.

2) Mr. X breached his fiduciary duty of loyalty to said investors.

3) Mr. X was negligent in his dealings with the investors.

4) Mr. X breached the investors' contracts.

5) Mr. X must pay back at least $13,000,000 to investors.

6) Accountants "R" Us committed fraud, negligence, and was guilty of negligent misrepresentation.

7) Accountants "R" Us is liable for $23,000,000 in damages.

As I enter the JR for one last time, the relief is palpable. Not wanting to lose track of what I've done, I gather my four steno pads- the ones the bailiff told us we cannot take with us- and stuff them in amongst my belongings. A few other jurors quickly do the same. My Scrabble game has been spirited off by Number One, the lady I did the most battle with. As I'm sitting there, gathering my wits, in comes the judge, sans god-like robe, looking like a normal human being.

"Thank you again for your unparalleled service."

"Thank you, judge," one of the lady jurors says as she presents him with a poster-sized Thank You card from all of us.

"This is the first time a jury has ever given me something like this," he says, a little choked up as he looks the card over. "Thank you so much."

Though enjoying the conversation, I want to get out of that room and clear of the courthouse before someone approaches and asks for my steno pads. I slink out into the hallway, trying to better secure my legal contraband, which now includes copies of the infamous jury instructions and verdict forms, not to mention the Juror badge. Several of the plaintiff's attorneys and staff are milling around by the elevator doors. Finally able to communicate with the very people I've been forbidden to go anywhere near for the last five weeks, I shake hands and talk to several of them. There's Mr. Stoneface, the lawyer who I'd not seen grin or crack one smile during the entire trial. He's beaming.

"It's a great thing you've done this day," he tells me. Other lawyers and assistants thank us profusely for our service.

Before I head down the stairs, I go back to the JR for a minute. Other jurors are finally leaving the room, going on and on about how interesting and friendly the judge was. It seems that he shared some personal information with them, at one point telling them how he'd served a mission for the Mormon Church. In the seventies. In Argentina, to be exact. At the same time and in the same area where I'd worked. So that's what being devious cost me- the opportunity to talk with him about that place where we'd both served.

Out onto the sidewalk we spill. Though there isn't a crowd of reporters fighting with each other for our words or photographs, there is one journalist there from the daily paper. He wants to speak to some of us. In a spare moment, when he's not talking to the jury foreman, I catch his attention.

"Is our verdict really the big deal those attorneys said it is?"

"I've been following Mr. X's shenanigans for years. You're the first jury to have brought this jerk to justice."

"Really. I had no idea."

"Your verdict assures that Mr. X will never be able to conduct business in this state again. You made history today."

The weather warm and beautiful, our group of worn-out jurists walks and talks its way to a bar and grill, where we gather chairs into a semi-circle on the sidewalk. We sit and eat and drink and revel in our new-found freedom and accomplishments- an odd mixture of release from bondage, coupled with the knowledge that we've done something good, even if that "good" is hard to quantify. But we share a camaraderie I've never experienced before. Usually jurors scatter as soon as they leave the courthouse, regardless of the intense times they've spent together. Not this group. We've been through so much that there's a bond holding us together- at least for the ten of us who voted for conviction. Numbers Two and Eight vanished the minute the trial ended.

As we sit there in the sunshine, reminiscing, one of the Canadian legal assistants approaches and joins the group. She becomes the first of a series of "insiders" who start filling in the blanks about all that went on behind the scenes- like the years of work that counsel for the investors put into nailing Mr. X and Accountants "R" Us. More bits and pieces are revealed when a legal assistant for the local firm happens to walk by. She's the person who came across an email so incriminating that she ran down the hall to show Galahad what she'd found. At that moment they realized they had a case against Mr. X and the accounting firm. I hope she got a large bonus.

She tells us that the lawyers had a nickname for each of us. Afflicted with a cold much of the time, I was known as "Sniffles."

Later I head for home, as I have one last Creative Writing class to attend. There are hugs and handshakes all around. And though I hate to leave, our duty is done. I feel a tremendous sense of accomplishment.

June 16

CIRCUIT COURT OF THE STATE OF XXXXXXX

Daniel Hiland

Dear. Mr. Hiland,

Thank you for your jury service on the --------------- trial. I appreciated having you in my court throughout the six weeks and understand the personal sacrifice you made to serve on this jury.

Your willingness to show up every morning for six weeks with a positive attitude is what made this trial possible. Without the involvement of citizens like you, the justice system would not function effectively.

I hope your jury term was a satisfying and valuable experience. On behalf of everyone involved, your service was truly appreciated.

Sincerely,

Paul XXXXXX

Circuit Court Judge

P.S. Thanks so much for being such a diligent juror over such a long period of time, and especially for being so understanding of my personal need to take some time off in the middle of the trial to be with my family.

July

Jurors:

The question has been posed to my clerks about communications regarding this trial after you have been discharged as jurors. The attorneys are not allowed to initiate contact with any of you and will respect your privacy. However, once you are discharged you are free to communicate with anyone regarding the trial.

Judge Paul XXXXXX

But there was one final detail to attend to. Something that made me wish I'd accepted the offer to be jury foreman …

Galahad Speaks

A COUPLE WEEKS AFTER THE TRIAL ENDED, I attended a special dinner. Jury consultants were footing the bill at one of the more expensive restaurants downtown. They wanted to pick our brains about the five-week experience we'd recently endured. A member of the plaintiff's law firm was there. So were Galahad and one of his assistant attorneys. It was good to see him again and be able to speak freely. As we ate, the group asked us questions: What was your view of the trial? How well did you understand what was going on? That second question made me a bit uncomfortable. Though I'd taken a ton of notes, I never did believe I had my mind totally wrapped around major details of the case.

One of the hot topics was the amount and complexity of the financial information we had to digest. This led to talk about the deliberation process. They were curious as to how we arrived at decisions about the damage amounts. Now, there'd always been some confusion about the verdict forms, which made it tough to figure out how much we should award to the plaintiffs. I recalled how frustrated I'd become during deliberations.

Some portions of those damned forms made no sense to me. But no one seemed willing to help me figure it out. I assumed it was because I lacked business sense or the requisite financial acumen. What I hadn't considered was that maybe, just maybe, most of the other jurors didn't know what the hell was going on either, none of them willing to admit as much.

We took turns explaining how we'd broken up the $40,000,000 award into smaller chunks. This was done, based on our understanding that the money had to be divided between the three different verdict scenarios. Then Galahad spoke up.

"But, you could have awarded the total amount on all three verdict forms."

Three verdict forms? As the import of his statement sunk in, some of the jurors groaned. Others swore. I felt ill. Because we hadn't asked enough questions of the judge during deliberations, we had shorted the plaintiffs two-thirds of what they had coming to them. Galahad, as he explained this little detail to us, didn't seem irritated. But I wondered what he thought of us. That was one big boatload of money. How could we have been so stupid? That was when I wondered how it might have all turned out if I'd been the foreman. I'm the type of person who, when faced with a puzzle, will keep asking questions until I understand the problem well enough to come to a solution. It may take me a long time to arrive at said solution, but I'll eventually get there. But second-guessing the foreman and laying the blame at his feet was a lame thing to do, as well. It wasn't like any of us were operating with full set of instructions. When a question arose, the foreman would contact the bailiff with the query scribbled on a piece of paper. The bailiff would carry this to the judge. Then we'd receive an answer. Sometimes the answer wasn't clear, so we'd ask again. But the judge could only give us so much help without appearing to be fiddling with the deliberation process. And considering the complexity of the case, it was a wonder we didn't screw up anything else. As I returned home later, I still felt a measure of shame. On the one hand, we'd made state history with our decision. On the other, we'd screwed up in a monumental way.

But our sins were small in comparison to those of Mr. X, whose initial post-trial objective was to get the hell out of town, and return to his palatial home in Florida. I saw nothing in the papers then, or for several years, about how much of the stolen funds he repaid. Much was made of the fact that he wasn't tried for embezzlement, but no answers were forthcoming- as if the damaged parties just wanted the whole affair to be over and done with so they could all move on.

Ever the ambitious fellow, Mr. X had one sole objective: to start making money again. In a repeat of his earlier M.O.- that of screwing over as many people as possible in a short period of time- Mr. X was busy during bilking investors of some $13,000,000. Falsely claiming that he owned shares in several Internet companies, he used at least $4,750,000 of the blood money to repay the investors he'd hosed years earlier. In a perverse way, he was trying to make restitution- but at the expense of yet more innocents, who lost another $1,500,000 to their friendly investor for travel expenses and personal use. And so it was that Mr. X was eventually taken into custody by some of the Sunshine state's finest. Within twelve weeks, he'd pled guilty in federal court to fraud, and then spent the remainder of the year in a detention facility. In December, a federal judge sentenced Mr. X to six years in federal prison. He'll be able to celebrate his 79th birthday as a free man.

Verdict

Friday, August 8

SO FAR, THIS HIDING OUT IS WORKING WELL. All I have to do is punch out at 3:30 and walk away. It would be more difficult if a lot of my acquaintances hadn't already preceded me. As it stands, there are few people remaining that I care to bid farewell to.

It's sort of strange to work for a place this long, then leave with no severance pay. No one begging me to stay. And not much in the way of thanks. Guess that's my reward for quitting. Some would say I'm running away from my problems, but that only applies if the problem can be solved and me still remain at work. But what I want and what The Company wants are two different things. So, there's only one solution: go someplace where work instructions are not considered a necessary evil. Some say this isn't so- that management is *behind* the effort to get SOPs for every operation, so that all employees can be successful at their jobs. Well, I don't buy it anymore. I've heard that out-of-tune song too many times.

Ten minutes to go.

And should I be sad and cry during these last few minutes? No. I've already done my crying. All those times when I slammed my office door too hard, or threw stuff across the office, or kicked a chair across the room, or was rude to others, or just cursed and cursed and beat my fists on the desktop until the tears came. But there are no tears left for this place. I can't afford to weep about leaving here, and even if I could manage to work up a few sniffles, what would be the point? Better to move on while I'm still employable. Five minutes.

Maybe at my next job I'll learn how to be a friend to others- one who isn't afraid to go for walks with co-workers, or share a lunch break, or even enjoy a party in my honor. For now, those are challenges I'm not willing to address. After fourteen years and four bosses, it's time to punch out. Goodbye to what was once a great job.

I walk downstairs and slide open the usually-locked glass window behind which all the employee photo ID cards are mounted, and remove mine- as a souvenir. I punch out and place my employee badge in the HR mail slot. Leaving by the East door, via the Punch Press area, I can avoid the lobby and any lingering questions the receptionist might have. I stop and take one last look at the building I spent fourteen years in- then walk past a couple of security guards, cross the street, kick over one of the safety cones that the Safety Lady put out there to keep us from legally parking on city streets, then get in my truck and drive away. It's good to see The Company in my rear-view mirror for the last time.

Appendix

The Early Cases

The Case of the Frozen Employees

Armed Robbery

October 6, 1980

I APPEARED FOR DUTY AS A JUROR at the downtown County Courthouse. Back then the standard length of service was two weeks. One hundred fifty of us were directed to an assembly room for orientation and registration. Soon they started calling names, mine not being one of them. My feelings at the time were mixed. If I was called, *fine*, but my understanding of all things legal limited to Perry Mason episodes, I was more apprehensive than anything else. Was there a school somewhere, college classes one could take? Nothing better to do than remain seated, I read for a while, got sleepy, played solitaire, napped, then read some more. They gave us two hours for lunch, much of which I spent nervously milling around.

But at 3:30 my name was called. Once our little band was chosen, we were ushered to a courtroom. Apparently, it was a trial for armed robbery. We found seats in the gallery while the first set of twelve potential jurors went to the box. As was their privilege, attorneys for plaintiff and defense questioned the candidates, the process called "voir dire." Queries ranged from occupation to prior experience in the courtroom to opinions about the justice system itself. And all the time the attorneys were analyzing the folks in the box: Would they be biased for or against the defendant? Were they competent to serve?

Eventually, the defense attorney issued six challenges for cause. Six jurors were thanked by the judge, then informed they'd been dismissed, no reason given. I was called to the box, the seat still warm. I had to endure the nerve-wracking experience of answering questions while the judge and everyone else in the room watched. But it was exciting to be there, a part of the proceedings, a part of the justice process. Sitting in that chair engendered a feeling of privilege and responsibility. Eventually my inquisition ended and the attorneys moved on to the next victim. It wasn't until the rest of the seats were filled and the questioning finished that I realized I was about to become a full-fledged juror. For one reason or another, the attorneys wanted our particular collection of citizens to judge the facts as they'd be presented. The judge swore us in as a group. We were now committed. There was no turning back.

The following morning, we all made our way to the courtroom and found our respective chairs in the jury box. The defendant, seated next to his attorney, was well dressed and groomed, in the diaphanously thin hope that his lawyer's tonsorial efforts would sway the jury. A court reporter perched over a strange-looking typewriter that noiselessly entered every spoken word at lightning speed. The prosecuting attorney sat at a different table, ready to go. The judge welcomed us back and repeated the jury instructions. Then he described the charges against the defendant.

Opening statements followed. First the prosecution spoke, giving us an outline of the case. The big picture established, he told us what he expected to prove and how. The defense attorney then got his turn, telling us his version of events. He told us his job was to make sure justice was done, but that he had a responsibility to protect his client, and that the defendant had rights, under the law, which should not be violated. Then came presentation of the evidence, the details about who did what, and to whom, as well as where and when it all occurred; upon this would be built a foundation for proof of intent to commit the alleged crime.

The defendant and two of his chums were accused of robbing a Skippers Fish and Chips Chowder House at gunpoint. I wondered where the other two were. Maybe their trials were over and done with. Regardless, the defendant and his buddies forced the kitchen staff into a walk-in freezer, then forced one of them to open the safe. While they were gathering the loot, a Skippers employee (who'd gotten off work earlier) was standing at a bus stop across the street. Having witnessed the whole thing going down. he called the police. Finished loading their ill-gotten gains, the trio fled in their getaway car. But since said vehicle was a total piece of crap, it broke down two blocks from the scene. The police were armed and waiting.

During presentation of the evidence, and subsequent objections and sustainings, tempers flared and arguments ensued between the lawyers. When things threatened to escalate too far, the judge would call these adversaries to his bench for a conversation, in low tones, about things the jury wasn't supposed to hear. If further discussion was warranted, the judge would invite the attorneys to his chambers.

The defense tried its best to convince us that the defendant was not guilty, but there was too much evidence to the contrary. After closing arguments, the judge instructed, then excused us to retreat to the jury room. A foreman was picked, the details discussed and we found the defendant guilty of 1st Degree Armed Robbery. We returned to the courtroom and the verdict was read. Though I wanted to hang around to see what happened next, the judge excused us. Back to the jury room we went, exiting from another door directly into the hallway.

Deciding to walk home rather than take the bus, I pondered what I'd seen and heard and felt as I plodded across a river bridge. I liked being a juror. Following an all-morning wait in the main assembly room the next day, we were sent home for the rest of the week.

Monday the 13th I was called to serve on a six-person jury, this time in District Court. We heard a case involving a female drunken driver. We found her guilty and were on our way home by 3:30 pm.

The Case of the Frightened Father

1st Degree Assault

October 16, 1980

ON THURSDAY I WAS CHOSEN for a criminal trial. An elderly man was accused of committing First Degree Assault. From the beginning, this case was different. And the more evidence we heard, the more it seemed as if the wrong person was on trial. The prosecution laid out the facts: that a woman's ex-husband called on a particular day and said he'd be stopping by her father's home (where she was staying) later that afternoon. When he did arrive, the woman's father (the defendant) shot him with a gun as he was about to enter the house, via the back door. The defense claimed that the defendant shot the plaintiff because he was in fear for the life of his daughter.

And so it began. The Prosecution said his client was the victim of an unwarranted attack- that the plaintiff had done nothing wrong on the day in question. But as the facts came out, we began to wonder. The defendant's attorney told us the tale of a terrified woman, a wife who'd been terrorized and beaten and harassed and stalked. Police reports told of the day the plaintiff was hauled off by the police after assaulting his wife; that he fought so hard he broke the restraints the police placed on him. On another occasion he chased the woman down (in traffic) and assaulted her again. Incident after incident was described by the defense. But the prosecution took pains to remind us that the woman's father, not his client, was the one on trial. Yet it was his client who was the bully, the stalker, the sadist. In short, a card-carrying sociopath.

At one point, after a particularly disturbing set of incidents was presented, prosecution had the plaintiff stand and pull his shirt up so we could see the healed-over bullet hole and surgical scars. The attorney had the man tell us how much he had suffered, had almost died, was on medication for the rest of his life. Blah, blah, blah. But there was no sympathy coming his way from the jury. We had heard too much. Or at least we thought we had.

One fine day the psycho told his ex that he'd had enough. On a particular date one year hence, he was going to kill her. The months passed. The stalking and harassment continued. The fear built. And then, on the very day, one year later, a phone rang at the defendant's house. It was Psycho. He wanted his ex-wife to know he'd be stopping by later that day for a "visit." And that was when the woman's father snapped. He got out his gun and proceeded to wait. And wait. And wait. Hours passed- and then there was a noise by the back porch. The old man looked out and saw Psycho approaching the door, carrying something in his hand which the father couldn't see through the screen. Psycho knocked on the door and said he was coming in. That was when the father opened fire. Then he called the police. Arriving officers found the victim lying on the porch, bleeding out from a stomach wound. The other thing they found was the bottle of pop he'd been holding in his hand. There was no gun, no other weapon. And with that the defendant's fate was sealed.

We retired to the jury room, facing a tough choice. On the one hand, the defendant fired at the victim because he feared for his family's life, especially that of his daughter. On the other, he took the law into his own hands. But what about the plaintiff? By all accounts he was one sick, violent bastard. He belonged in prison. And what of the father? He had all day to think about the implications of his actions. He could have called the cops anytime during those long hours leading up to the violent act. Then they would have been there waiting. But what good had police involvement been in the past? Despite repeated arrests and detainment, Psycho continued to return, like a living nightmare.

We argued back and forth about the evidence. Yes, we'd heard a lot about Psycho's dirty deeds. But he wasn't the one on trial. And the record showed that when faced with the option to call the police, the old man instead took the law into his own hands. What should we do? Disregard the evidence and in essence, take the law into our own hands by ignoring our duty?

After an hour we took our first vote. Each of us wrote "guilty" or "not guilty" on a scrap of paper and handed it to the foreman. We were several votes short of the requisite ten. We talked some more- about how taking the law into one's hands was not something that civilized societies were built upon. We voted again. Ten to convict, two to acquit. Pressing the buzzer, the foreman summoned the bailiff. We were ready. We filed through the door and back to our seats, the defendant and his wife standing over by the Defense table. The verdict was read and the man's wife started crying. And we were then excused from the room, the curtain closing before we could watch the final scene unfold.

We said little to each other as we gathered our coats and bags and other belongings. We walked out of the jury room and down the stairs and out the door, mostly in silence. Justice had been served. But it didn't feel right. No, not right at all...

The Case of the Flying Pedestrian

DUI, Hit and Run, 2nd Degree Assault

January 1989

THE CALL TO SERVE AGAIN ARRIVED. Another bus ride downtown for the 8 am appointment. More waiting with a large, diverse crowd in the assembly room. This time around we were treated to a boring 20-minute film about jury service, then endured a two-hour wait while the preliminaries were dispensed with. Then the Calling of the Names ensued. Around 11 am I heard mine announced through the loudspeaker. Up to the third floor we climbed, then assumed the position in the gallery.

I thought about how much had changed in my life since last serving. I was now married to a good woman, having escaped the hell of single life. I was a father. I had a decent job. On the other hand, the courthouse looked the same. The worn flooring and carpets, the polished wooden banisters, the ancient doors and bathroom fixtures, the faded curtains and off-white ceiling tiles. I felt like a veteran juror by this time, but that air of uncertainty persisted. Like I said, some things don't change.

I was the second juror called forth to the judicial hot seat. After surviving voir dire and challenges for cause, during which four jurors were sent packing, the rest of us were sworn in and the trial began: a complicated hit-and-run case.

Once upon a midnight bleary, Mr. Perez exited a bar, apparently in a questionable state of sobriety. Getting into his vehicle, which we'll call Car A, Perez commenced driving up a one-way street the wrong way, at which time he smashed head-on into Car B. Deciding it was time to change direction, Perez beat a hasty retreat, thus smashing into Car C. Then Perez stopped the car to consider his options. Car B pulled across the street and parked.

Meanwhile, a fourth vehicle (Car D) arrived, driven by a woman who decided to stop and be a witness. She and her hubby were parked across the street. The three drivers got out and began inspecting the damage. An argument ensued. Perez, upon hearing that the police were on their way, beat feet to his car and started to take off. The man from Car D got in front of Car A and told Perez to stop, while a lady bartender tried unsuccessfully to grab Perez' keys out of the ignition.

Undaunted, Mr. Perez stomped on the gas pedal. Car A then lurched forward, flinging the man from Car D onto its hood. Perez drove about ten feet, then stopped. He'd had enough, and began yelling at the man from Car D to get off his blankety-blank hood. But before the fellow was all the way clear, Perez gunned it, taking his human hood ornament for a joyride of several blocks.

For all his faults- and there are many- Mr. Perez deserves an "A" for effort. He swerved. He zig-zagged. He cursed. But regardless, he couldn't shake the man from Car D. At the entrance to another one-way street, Perez slammed on the brakes, sending his uninvited passenger flying. Upon landing, the former hood passenger looked up in time to see Car A heading straight for him. He rolled out of the way at the last second. Undaunted and clueless, Car A continued its trip up the one-way street. In the wrong direction, of course.

Time passed. A policeman passing a convenience store noticed someone inside, pushing the clerk around. It was Perez. Calling for assistance, said officer pulled into the store parking lot just as Perez decided to stop hitting the clerk and start hitting the bricks. A K9 unit being the first on the scene, one of the dogs picked up the scent and tracked Perez to a yard three blocks from the store, where it kept him pinned to the ground until officers arrived.

Off to the jury room we went to consider all that had happened during Perez' big night out. It would have been easy, had he only been accused of a DUI. But no, he had to try and run over someone, as well. We had to determine the defendant's guilt on four counts:

1) Driving under the influence
2) Vehicular hit-and-run
3) Hit-and-run with injury to a person
4) 2nd Degree Assault

The first three counts were easy to confirm. It was a question of whether or not the assault was *intentional* that had us confused. A two-hour discussion ensued. Was the assault intentional or was Perez merely reckless? We voted once. 9 to 3. We talked. We voted again. Same result. More talk. We voted a third time. Still 9 to 3. Fed up, I spoke at length to the recalcitrant juror. While I don't remember what I said about Perez' actions being intentional, I finally got through. Before we made a final decision, though, we made a request of the judge for some clarification. We were asked to return to the courtroom, where the judge recited the degrees of Assault, as found in the state criminal code.

Back in the jury room, we voted one more time and that doubt-filled juror decided to vote "Guilty." The bailiff was summoned and we returned to the courtroom for the reading of the verdict. Case closed.

The Case of the Wayward Drill

Negligence and Malpractice

January 1989

SIX DAYS AFTER THE PEREZ TRIAL, I was chosen as juror for a civil action involving dental malpractice: a root canal gone wrong. Excited about the prospect of being involved in what appeared to be a complex case, for a change, I nearly disqualified myself during voir dire. I set the tone right from the beginning.

Plaintiff's attorney approached me.

"So, your last name is Hiland, that's correct, isn't it?"

"Yes."

"Are you Scottish?" she asked.

I thought for a moment. Then-

"No. Not yet."

Laughter erupted in the courtroom.

Everyone likes a good laugh now and then, but the trouble with trying to be funny in the courtroom is that:

a) Regardless of how well you think you've worked the crowd, you're never quite sure if they're laughing *with* or *at* you.

b) Unlike you, these lawyer types have heard it all before, and judging from the wicked sense of humor they possess, you're probably in, way over your head.

To not risk looking like a total jackass, I decided to cut back on the amusing repartee and stick to the facts. But the attorney wasn't done with me.

"So, tell me, Mr. Hiland. What's the most painful experience in your life?"

A fast-forward reel of possible examples flashed through my mind. Being attacked by a swarm of yellow jackets. Landing face-first on the pavement when the front tire popped off my bike. Smashing my right hand with a fence post pounder. Breaking same hand while pounding a box in anger. Stepping on a nail while wearing thongs in a barnyard. No. No. None of these. Sensing the opportunity of a lifetime- a chance to really slay the audience- I cast aside my resolution to avoid levity, in favor of laughs.

"Well, several years ago I needed some dental work done. It was an emergency. I let the dentist drill on me without Novocain."

The response was immediate and loud. On a roll, I gave several more answers, eliciting additional chuckles from the troops. I felt like the world's greatest comedian. Maybe I could go on tour as the "Dan, the Funny Juror."

So flushed with success was I that I couldn't focus on the attorney's follow-up question about pain. I asked her to repeat the query. Then I asked if she would explain it.

Then I stumbled and fumbled, before finally understanding what she was after. But the party was over. The attorney moved on, leaving me a nervous wreck. The king of comedy was officially dead. And with his demise, had my smartass remarks also taken me out of the running as a juror? I wanted to be part of this trial in the worst way- knowing it was going to be a complicated ten-day mess, but also out of curiosity. The defendant was a member of The Church of Jesus Christ of Latter-day Saints, just like me. He was also a "stake president," a high-profile position that involved a lot of responsibility. How could this have happened to a "respectable" individual like himself? How would he comport himself during the trial? And, how would I?

Once thing I didn't have to worry about was finances. My employer would be footing the bill for this ten-day trial, so I was technically on vacation. But I wasn't holding my breath. Convinced that my recent court performance under questioning had scuttled any chances of being selected as a juror, I offered up a prayer. The day ended without a jury being empaneled.

The next morning brought another thirty minutes of voir dire. During questioning of one of the last two original jurors, the prosecuting attorney had an emotional meltdown. The judge then sent our pool of candidate's off to the jury room while the sobbing lawyer composed herself. As I discovered later, this was only the first of what would be several attempts by prosecution to manipulate jury emotion. Once back in the courtroom, the real fun began: peremptory challenges. While challenges for cause- meaning a quick exit for any juror- can be unlimited in number, peremptories are usually limited to six. But I wasn't aware of the statutory limit. All I knew was that every time the court clerk carried a slip of paper to the judge's bench, a juror disappeared. First went a juror two seats away. Then someone on my right. When would my name be uttered? One, two, three, four more were excused as I sat there like a plastic duck in a carnival firing range. Then they were done. I sat there, astounded at my luck. I was in. But then the judge called us to attention.

"Before you're all sworn in as jurors, I have one last question."

Oh hell, here it comes...

"Do any of you have strong feelings or issues with the fact that the defendant is a high-ranking member of the LDS Church?"

Of all the question to ask. As I thought about it, I felt the eyes of everyone in the courtroom on me and my fellow jurors-to-be. It was as if the word "MORMON" were emblazoned across my forehead in bright red letters. But I'd already given the issue some thought. It didn't matter who the defendant was, or who he was related to, or what his religious affiliation was. If he'd broken the law or violated someone's rights, he should be held accountable. My conscience calm on that issue, I also resolved that for the next ten days I would not breathe a word about my being LDS to anyone in that courthouse.

The moments of dreadful silence past, we were asked to stand. The judge swore us in. After two alternate jurors were called up and sworn, one of them was excused and replaced.

And so it began. Attorney for the plaintiff (who I will hereafter refer to as Mrs. Tooth, or simply Tooth), stood and gave her opening remarks. Her client accused the defendant (who I will hereafter refer to as Dr. Drill), of performing a bad root canal. After botching the surgery, he sent her on her way. While on vacation she incurred terrible post-op complications that caused her much pain and suffering.

As Tooth's lawyer explained the details via long stretches of dialog, the judge started nodding off. The bailiff rattled some desk drawers, but to no avail. Then she ascended to the judge's chambers, slamming the door behind her as she went. Suddenly the adjudicator's eyes popped open. Opening remarks for the plaintiff at an end, we were excused for a two-hour lunch break. Down the street I ran, a good ten blocks to Burger King for lunch with Carol and our daughter. It was good to see them, after all the depressing things I'd been listening to.

Opening statements by the defense were next. Dr. Drill's attorney looked to be a tough customer. Short and a bit stocky, his slicked-back, dark hair gave him a Mafia look. His intense delivery style made me understand why he'd been chosen for this case; he was there to defend his client, come hell or higher water.

Mrs. Tooth was called to the stand, but partway through her testimony, she broke down in tears. The judge called a halt to the proceedings and sent us home for the rest of the day.

By Friday we all had the big picture, at least from Tooth's point of view. So far, we'd learned that Mrs. Tooth went to Dr. Drill for a root canal. He began the procedure. At some point the patient said she experienced a horribly sharp pain in her jaw that made her jump. She told the doctor as much. He said not to worry, and didn't appear too concerned. On the procedure went, with the drilling and the scraping required to remove the rest of the root. Medication was applied and gutta-percha inserted to fill the empty space. Finally, the temporary cap was attached. Dr. Drill gave his patient instructions about what to do and expect, prior to a return appointment two weeks later.

Off Mrs. Tooth went, on vacation to Idaho. A day or two later, during a meal, the temporary came loose and fell off. Mrs. Tooth contacted Dr. Drill and was given instructions about not getting any more food in the hole until it could be closed again.

By the time she returned home, many days later, she was in terrible pain and had to be referred to a specialist. Before long she had been to an endodontist, a nerve specialist and others. It was discovered that the lower portion of the affected tooth had been perforated by a drill, during the root canal procedure. Unaware of this, the doctor had packed gutta-percha into the tooth anyway, some of the filler material extruding out of the back of the tooth, into the gums and other places it didn't belong. Infection set in and at some point, Mrs. Tooth experienced paresthesia- a paralysis of the side of her face, due to nerve damage. Her attorney was seeking $1,800,000 in damages. Also mentioned in the suit was another $20,000 for loss of consortium, a euphemism for cessation of sexual activity. I decided to ponder that little detail some other time, like maybe a few years after the trial ended.

It took the better part of three days to get through all the testimony, the gory details, the angst of the plaintiff. Along the way, I got queasy; at one point I even developed a tooth ache. Was this my body's way of manifesting sympathetic symptoms in reaction to all the dental horror I'd been exposed to in the courtroom? Would the trial have to be delayed so I could receive some emergency dental work of my own? After a couple days of worry and pain, I discovered the problem. A popcorn shell had lodged itself between a molar and gums- from that popcorn sold in the little courthouse store in the front lobby.

I'd amassed twenty pages of notes based on testimony given by Mrs. Tooth, other witnesses and the visual aids presented by Tooth's lawyer. But due to some specific objections raised- and in some cases sustained by Drill's attorney- I was beginning to wonder how much at fault the doctor really was.

The following Tuesday it was Drill's turn. For the next two days we got to hear how Mrs. Tooth went on her trip, when the temporary came off, and other details. We were told that Mrs. Tooth ignored Dr. Drill's advice and went on eating with that hole in her tooth exposed; how food probably got packed in the with the gutta-percha, thus aggravating an already bad situation; how she delayed returning to the doctor for treatment. And again we went through the gory details, but now from the point of view of a dentist whose advice had been ignored.

The defense finished, Drill's attorney talked to us about contributory negligence: a situation that occurs when plaintiff's own negligence contributes to (aggravates) the damage they have suffered. The attorney reminded us that while deliberating about damage amounts, we needed to keep in mind how much pain and suffering Mrs. Tooth's negligent behavior caused her, apart from anything the doctor could be blamed for.

On to closing arguments we went. Tooth's attorney went first, then Drill's. Then Mrs. Tooth's lawyer piped up once more, finishing her remarks with this little gem:

"Remember when the injury occurred, folks. Two-thirty in the afternoon. *Tooth-hurty.*"

What the hell? Was this supposed to be funny? We didn't think so, and said as much upon returning to the jury room to deliberate. Various words and phrases were used to describe her: jackass; bitch; stupid bitch, etc.

We elected a foreman, in this case an accountant. Then the talking began. We were to decide several things:

1) To what degree, if any, was Dr. Drill negligent in his treatment of Mrs. Tooth?

2) Did Mrs. Tooth ignore his instructions about post-surgery care? If so, to what extent did these actions contribute to her subsequent health problems?

3) Was there a lack of consortium, as it related to Mr. and Mrs. Tooth? If so, was it worth $20,000?

Our discussions took the better part of three days, during which time we talked and we talked and we talked. We'd take breaks for lunch, then return. And at the end of the day we'd tell the bailiff to let the judge know that we weren't ready yet. But we did arrive at some conclusions:

1) The doctor was negligent, in that having done root canals for a living, he should have recognized when some part of his procedure was going wrong.

2) Mrs. Tooth shared in the negligence by not following her doctor's orders. Her choice caused her unnecessary pain and suffering, as well as other costly treatments.

3) How much "consortium" could be going on between two folks in their mid-seventies? Not wanting to dwell on the possibilities, we denied that award to the plaintiffs.

In the end, we found Dr. Drill 75% negligent, with Mrs. Tooth assuming the other 25% as contributory.
But we still had to figure out the damage amount. And when the foreman asked us about $1.8 million dollars, he

drew blank stares. He suggested we start small. Say $20,000, then work our way up. We finally arrived at a consensus, or so we thought: $400,000. That seemed fair, taking everything into consideration- which wasn't easy, as twisty as this case seemed.

So, we voted. Less than ten agreed on the amount. We discussed things and voted again. Natch. After another attempt or two it came down to nine of us vs one woman. She was holding out for $500,000. Several hours passed as one juror after another tried to convince her that we had good reasons for the lesser amount. But she wouldn't budge. Out of frustration, several of us laid into her, wanting to know why she was holding out, her reasons more emotional than logical. I told her that we'd all compromised to reach the position we were at, so why couldn't she do the same? For whatever reason, she changed her mind and the foreman called the bailiff. We were done.

Made in United States
Orlando, FL
11 November 2026

90609395R00102